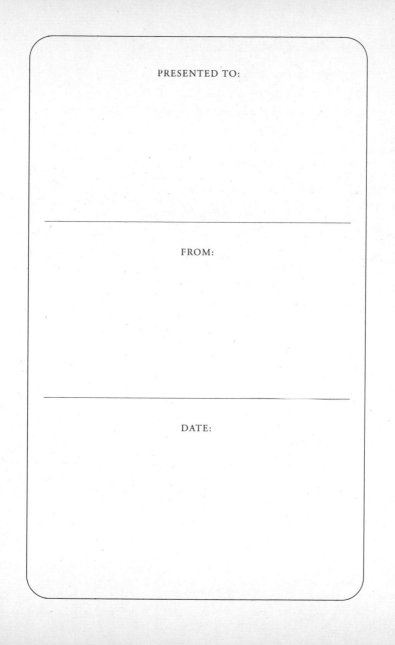

PRESENTED TO:

_____

FROM:

_____

DATE:

Other books by Michele Howe

Prayers to Nourish a Woman's Heart
Pilgrim Prayers for Single Moms
Going It Alone: Meeting the Challenges
  of Being a Single Mom

Forthcoming books by Michele Howe

Prayers of Comfort and Strength
Prayers for New and Expecting Moms

Prayers

for

Homeschool Moms

Prayers
for
Homeschool Moms

Michele Howe

JOSSEY-BASS
A Wiley Imprint
www.josseybass.com

Published by Jossey-Bass
A Wiley Imprint
989 Market Street, San Francisco, CA 94103-1741   www.josseybass.com

Jossey-Bass books and products are available through most bookstores. To contact Jossey-
Bass directly call our Customer Care Department within the U.S. at 800-956-7739, outside
the U.S. at 317-572-3986 or fax 317-572-4002.

Jossey-Bass also publishes its books in a variety of electronic formats. Some content that
appears in print may not be available in electronic books.

Unless otherwise noted, the Scripture quotations contained herein are from the New
American Standard Bible®, Copyright © 1960, 1962, 1963, 1968, 1971, 1973, 1975,
1977, 1995 by The Lockman Foundation. Used by permission. (www.Lockman.org)

Library of Congress Cataloging-in-Publication Data
Howe, Michele.
Prayers for homeschool moms / Michele Howe.–1st ed.
p. cm.
Includes bibliographical references.
ISBN 0-7879-6557-X (alk. paper)
1. Mothers–Prayer-books and devotions–English. 2. Home
schooling–Prayer-books and devotions–English. I. Title.
BV4847.H67 2003
242'.6431–dc21   2002155960

FIRST EDITION
HB Printing   10 9 8 7 6 5 4 3 2 1

Contents

Part Three
Character Development   63

Part Four
Challenges and Choices   95

To my homeschooling family—
To my husband Jim, who pursues excellence in every task
he undertakes.
To my children Nicole, Katlyn, Corinne, and Jamey,
who have patiently accompanied me on this homeschooling
adventure and make me proud to be called Mom.

Acknowledgments

Homeschooling, to the delight of many and the chagrin of a few, is an impressive movement that will not be pushed by the wayside. In the dozen years that I have been homeschooling my children, I have been blessed by the goodwill of countless professional and private homeschooling organizations. Whether I needed information, advice, or just a good dose of reassurance, help abounded. Homeschooling families face unique challenges, and perhaps that's the reason those who are a part of this group are so willing to lend a hand to others around them. It's an honor to work with these tremendously committed and gifted individuals, and I thank God for their influence upon my life. I would be hard pressed to say who has learned more in our homeschool, my children or me. I am sure, however, that without the unwavering support of my family and friends, I would have despaired long ago!

My most heartfelt thanks and appreciation also go to Mark Kerr, my editor at Jossey-Bass, who delighted me with his enthusiasm for this project. His excitement and experience transformed an elusive concept into a tangible reality. I am again honored to be associated with Mark and his team at Jossey-Bass, which includes Andrea Flint, production editor; Sandy Siegle, marketing manager; and Paula Goldstein, director, creative services. It does my soul good to work with professionals whose hearts are as generous as theirs.

My prayer is that this compilation of stories and prayers will reach every homeschooling mom exactly at her point of need, embracing her with hopeful encouragement and a sense of community. We're all on this parenting journey together. Let's make the most of the opportunities afforded us to do good whenever we're able.

Prayers
for
Homeschool Moms

PART ONE

The Practice of Homeschooling

$\mathcal{T}$he venture into homeschooling is a life-changing event. For moms whose children were previously educated outside the home in a public or private school, the adjustments may feel dramatic at times. For mothers who homeschool from the beginning, the challenges will include learning how to juggle home management and mothering along with the day-to-day educational instruction. In whatever circumstance your family finds itself, remember that moms and dads learn right along with their children. The learning curve never ends . . . and this is good. Enjoy the process while you plot your family's educational course and delight in the wonders of discovery side by side with your family.

One Step at a Time

Perusing the bookshelves of friends' homes had become a hobby for Cassie. Ever since she and her husband Kurt decided that the private school their daughter attended wasn't meeting the needs of their child in the way they'd hoped, Cassie had scoured around for any book she could find on homeschooling. Since two of her closest friends had homeschooled from day one, Cassie knew where to go for both emotional and practical support. Still, Cassie felt the burden of developing a well-rounded educational curriculum fall heavily upon her shoulders. Although Kurt agreed that homeschooling sounded like a viable option, he didn't feel he had the time to do the necessary research. So the bulk of the responsibility fell to Cassie to set up the new program before the holidays were over.

Beginning January 16, Cassie would be the teacher. Her part-time position as the school librarian gave her plenty of know-how in locating needed resources. Yet Cassie lacked experience in organizing a doable system in the practicalities of educating her daughter. She would most definitely need the assistance of her good friends. Some days as Cassie poured over various catalogs she felt overwhelmed by the sheer number of supplies on the market. A quick call to a friend usually calmed her down. But even though Cassie and Kurt believed that home educating, at least for the remainder of the year, would prove beneficial to their daughter, Cassie still nursed niggling doubts in the back of her mind. After one especially difficult afternoon of planning, Cassie retreated to her enclosed porch with Bible in one hand and journal in the other. Right now I'm going to do business with God. I'm not getting up until I put on paper every reason we have for homeschooling. When the next bout of doubts comes calling, I'll be ready.

For I am confident of this very thing, that He who began a good work in you will perfect it until the day of Christ Jesus.
—PHILIPPIANS 1:6

Dear Lord, I must come before you in the deepest gratitude for I finally understand that you are the sole provider of my strength. Any confidence that I might possess stems directly from you. Thank you for graciously giving me the courage I require to take this momentous step. It's a rare thing for me to enter into unknown territory. There are moments, many of them quite frankly, when I am paralyzed by a sudden fear that leaves me frozen. I'm not certain I'm up to this challenge of educating my child. Yet there is another part of me that recognizes that you equipped me to parent my family even in this new way. I believe that you are able to teach me as I begin instructing my youngster. Thank you for the knowledge you have given me. I would ask that you continue to guide our steps and that we would bring honor to your name in all that we do. This new phase of life will usher in joy I'm sure. I come to you, Father, rejoicing that as parents we have this option. Thank you for placing us here, at this time, when so many others are choosing this same road upon which to travel. Let me be humble enough to seek out the help I'll require. And encourage me to seek out assistance when need be. Restrain in me attitudes of pride and self-sufficiency that may hinder my abilities to best influence my family. I commit my loved ones once again into your faithful hands. Be with me, give me your good words of wisdom, and instruct me in the way I should go. Amen.

The intelligence we have is a gift from God; the circumstances in which we find ourselves he controls. Obviously, we have to bring our intelligence as well as our faith to bear on those circumstances.

—ELISABETH ELLIOT IN *God's Guidance*

2
Self-Imposed Stress

*A*na, mom to Derek, felt her eyes begin to cross. They'd already spent the last forty-five minutes drilling phonic sounds from Derek's beginning reader. At seven years old, Derek still wasn't grasping even the basics of reading. He wasn't able to capture the sounds correctly, or if he did, the information was forgotten by the following day. Ana was getting desperate. How many times had she endured listening to other moms tell her that their youngster was already reading "chapter books"? Ugh. Try as she might, Ana couldn't get Derek past the first lesson or two of their home reading program. She started and stopped and started again. If Ana described herself as frustrated, then Derek was almost out of his mind. For the first time in his short life, Derek felt something was really wrong with him. He worried that he would never learn to read. Derek felt his mother's irritation with him but was powerless to change it. All in all, it was a no-win scenario.

After a full six months of daily "reading" lessons that had progressed nowhere, Ana gave up. She finally listened to that still, small voice inside her head. She decided to give it a rest for a time. The next morning when school started, Derek dejectedly reminded his mom that they hadn't done reading yet. Ana explained that for a while she was trading places with Derek. Puzzled, Derek asked for an explanation. Ana told her son that everyone could use some brushing up on reading skills . . . so she would be reading aloud to him every day. Derek's eyes widened. "Really?" he asked. Delighted with this new plan, Derek hurried into his room and retrieved an armful of his childhood favorites. Together, Ana and Derek read to their heart's delight. And for the first time in many days, both shared a smile.

Knowledge makes arrogant, but love edifies.
—1 CORINTHIANS 8:1

Dear Lord, I must come before you confessing my prideful heart. I've been so focused on making certain that my child is able to do what other children can do that I've hurt him. He is not ready for the skills I'm pressuring him to master. In my heart, I've known for quite a while that it's not time yet. Still, I've pressed him and frustrated him as well. This is wrong. Help me, Father, to not give in to peer pressure. Goodness, I wanted to homeschool my child to get away from society's ideas of educating according to someone else's standards. Here I am falling into the same trap I so wanted to avoid. And I've exasperated my beloved child in the process. Looking back, I can hardly believe I've allowed it to go this far. Instead of nurturing a love for reading and learning into my youngster, I've probably done just the opposite. Whoever said that homeschoolers were immune to peer pressure were certainly mistaken. I've just come to realize that no matter where I teach my child, I must guard my heart against the temptation to see his successes or failures as reflecting my competence as a mother and a teacher. I understand that I must be diligent in my lessons. Yet my mother's heart tells me that he is not ready for this challenge yet. My job is to creatively make learning appealing to him, even if it means that I must sacrifice some of my own well-formulated plans and take it one day at a time. Lord, continue to teach me to look into my own heart so that I might become the loving and joyful instructor you desire me to be. I trust in your guidance to help keep me on the right path. I depend upon your Holy Spirit to speak softly to my heart. Let my words bring encouragement, let my face reveal the love I feel. Amen.

A positive mom, generally speaking, is a smiling mom.
—KAROL LADD IN *The Power of a Positive Mom*

3

Standing Appointment

Thirty-six-year-old Tracy was mother to twin daughters age ten. Before Tracy ever married, she had become interested in the whole idea of homeschooling. As a former special education teacher at the local public school, Tracy understood how a small tutorial approach to education could be far superior to a class ratio of thirty to one. She also recognized throughout her stint as a public educator that as she worked one-on-one with her students she was able to tailor each child's assignments to his or her particular needs and abilities. No doubt, Tracy mused, this is the same approach I want to use when I have my own children. Some years later, Tracy and her husband Tim made the decision to home educate their daughters. It had been five years now, and Tracy was quite satisfied with her daughters' progress.

Yet there was one snag. Tim, who traveled several days each week out of the state, repeatedly expressed a desire to become more active in his children's education as well. But how would this ever work? Tracy schooled the girls from 9:00 A.M. until 2:00 P.M. each weekday. Tim's work schedule never allowed him to plan more than a few weeks in advance. Tracy mulled the problem over and finally came up with a workable solution. Since history was Tim's strong suit, they decided to implement a novel method for Tim to take over teaching this subject. Every day, at the same time, no matter where Tim was, he either called or e-mailed his girls. He would look over their work for the upcoming week before he left, and he always carried both a workbook and the teacher's edition with him. Then via the wonderful world of computer technology, Tim would ask his daughters questions and alternately they would either write out their essay replies on the computer or give him verbal explanations over the telephone. Even though it took some planning, Tim always looked forward to his half-hour of "teaching time" with his girls. Tracy was thrilled that not only was Tim keeping a pulse on the children's educational progress, but he was also investing in his daughters' lives on a day-to-day basis.

You, therefore, who teach one another, do you not teach your-self?
—ROMANS 2:21

Dear Lord, I am in awe of the marvelous methods you employ to work out our problems. We came before you asking for a solution to a small problem. It was no earth-shattering issue. Yet you were able to give us a novel way to solve it. Thank you, Lord. I give you praise for who you are as my heavenly father and my instructor. I am amazed that you care so much for even the smallest of my concerns. I'm also astounded by how much I've learned as I've become my children's teacher. Since we've taken on the responsibility of educating our children, I have witnessed your gracious provision time after time. On days when I do not have the strength or the desire to open another book, you are ready to lend me a hand. I can even sense your strength and good purpose course through me when I come to you for help. How would I ever accomplish this task without you? I dare not even contemplate it! You have been so very faithful to us. I ask that you continue to instruct me as I attempt to be a wise and diligent parent. Continue to infuse my mind with the words that will incite a love for learning in my children's hearts. Help me see the great privilege I have as a parent to impart life skills and lessons to my family. Mold and remake me; never stop instructing me as a parent, I beg. Help me set aside the nonessential and concentrate on what lasts throughout eternity. Lord, at times this task seems so daunting. Our schedule alone is often so complicated that I wonder how we'll accomplish all that we've set out to do. Lord, in this, give us your thoughts too. Show us the way when there doesn't seem to be any clear answer. Again, I am so grateful that you are always with us. Let our family bring honor to you today. Amen.

Be a student in some kind of class.
—H. Jackson Brown Jr. and Rosemary C. Brown
   in *Life's Little Instructions from the Bible*

4
Ready, Set, Test!

A newcomer to the oft-overwhelming world of home schooling, Cindy was experiencing more doubts on this day than any other previous. Prompted by a few friends who were veteran homeschoolers, Cindy was trying to decide whether to test her children at year's end. Some of the moms she conversed with pointed out the peace of mind that comes along with administering the SAT or ACT tests to the children on a yearly basis. It provides a gauge of sorts, helps a mom know where each child's strengths or weaknesses lay. But Cindy worried, what if the tests reveal major weaknesses? How will I summon up the courage to continue homeschooling next fall? And how exactly does one "test" one's own kids? Before Cindy could work through that daunting issue, a totally different opinion on testing was set forth by some other moms. "Don't test at all," they cried. "Why do you need someone else's standard to tell you what you already know? It's just a waste of time and standardized testing gives in to the whole 'secular' worldview of what's valued. Don't do it, Cindy," they warned.

After listening silently to a rather heated exchange between these opposing camps, Cindy was even more confused. Why did I open my mouth, she wondered. What puzzled Cindy most was how opinionated each mother seemed to be. Every one (excluding herself) had a voice in the matter . . . and made it known. Cindy then realized that it was probably good that these mothers did have such strong sentiments because she'd heard every one of them tell stories of how they'd had to defend their school of choice on countless occasions. Maybe, Cindy decided, taking issue, if done with respect, wasn't such a bad thing. For sure, Cindy knew she'd be welcome within this group of fiercely proactive moms whatever choice she eventually made. On her way out, Cindy received pats on the back and promises to pray for her as she decided. "Either way," one mom confided, "you can always change your mind next year. It's one of the benefits of being both mom and teacher."

Make my joy complete by being of the same mind maintaining the same love, united in spirit, intent on one purpose. Do nothing from selfishness or empty conceit, but with humility of mind let each of you regard one another as more important than yourself.
—PHILIPPIANS 2:2–3

Dear Lord, each and every day I am learning something new about this venture called homeschooling. I'm most definitely still riding the upper edge of the learning curve. Today was yet another good example when I felt completely out of my element. But as I followed the conversation and paid attention to the arguments posed, I came away with new insight. True enough, my friends and their strong opinions did surprise me. Still, I understand why they have developed certain viewpoints. They've all had to defend their positions on every aspect of home educating so many times that they've learned to be prepared. I can learn from them. I realized that no matter what decision I make on this particular issue, I need to gather the facts, organize the information, and then be courageous enough to stand behind it. Not that I won't make mistakes, but I can see that there is a mind-set I must develop. Help me learn how to sift through the myriad voices I hear. Give me the wisdom to discern between what is good and what is best for my family. Make my senses keen and my responses gracious, yet honest. Lord, I am not certain of the many turns in the road this homeschooling will take us. It does give me reason to pause and hesitate. Yet I am confident that as I seek your guidance and learn from the experiences of others who are farther along this road than I, all will be well. I give you thanks for your readiness to hear my cries of distress and how quickly you bring in the troops to assist me. Help me this day recognize what a stalwart group of supporters I have in my fellow homeschooling moms. They bring my heart joy and reassurance even if they do overwhelm with me their zeal at times. Amen.

We must decide if we will impress people or have an impact on them.
—JUD WILHITE IN *Faith That Goes the Distance*

5

Mind Games

With furrowed brow, Angie sat holding a stack of three-by-five-inch index cards and trying valiantly to place the single Bible verse in her memory. "Ack! Why is this so hard?" Angie moaned. Line by line, after approximately thirty grueling minutes, Angie had it down. Just to make sure she didn't lose the precious words to the tangle of other thoughts pushing for preeminence, Angie removed the card from the stack and placed it over her kitchen sink. Now, that's the ticket, Angie thought, satisfied. Goodness knows I spend enough time standing here doing dishes and preparing meals, I'll just take a quick glance every time I'm in the room. For the remainder of the day, Angie was as good as her word. During each task that took her into the kitchen, Angie made certain that she paused for a quick review of the verse she had committed to memory.

Beyond what she had expected, Angie actually started enjoying this little ritual of hers. Keeping a biblical promise in her thoughts throughout the day really did make a difference. When she became irritated at her son's laziness, she inwardly recited a verse on restraining one's anger. After Angie's daughter left her habitual trail of clothes and books strewn over the floors of the house, Angie called upon a verse that spoke of communicating with kindness. It didn't seem to matter what Angie was facing on any given day, calling up the verses from memory put a pleasant spin on her family's attitudes and actions. After about six months of committing one new verse per week to memory, Angie's stack of cards had grown . . . and so had she. *If God's word has affected my life like this, think how my kids will benefit too. It's my responsibility to get these youngsters to hide God's good word in their own hearts,* Angie determined. Not only will they have the tools to counteract bad thinking but their reservoir of hope will soar as well.

Set your minds on things above, not on the things that are on earth. For you have died and your life is hidden with Christ in God.
—Colossians 3:2–3

Dear Lord, my mind, my thoughts, my attitudes, all are of consequence to you. Though I sometimes attempt to hide what is inside my heart from others, you already know what I'm experiencing. Lord, I never want to be ashamed of what I'm thinking. Yet in truth, many of my thoughts are self-centered and defensive. I am continually guarding myself from pain. Help me, Lord. Begin a transformation within my mind. Remake me into the woman of grace you desire me to be. I've witnessed how taking single promises, one by one, found in your word has changed me. This should not surprise me and yet I never realized how a simple shift in focus could turn a disastrous situation into one with a glorious outcome.

I am also learning how very powerful your words are. This, too, astounds me. I stand in awe of the difference this minimal effort has made in our family. No longer are we quick to react, we are slowly learning to pause and think—and decide whether we really want to make an angry retort. Our conversations are far more uplifting than ever before. And I've witnessed my dear children actually compliment one another from a sincere heart. Thank you, Lord. These changes can only come from your abundant goodness. Continue, I pray, to work this ongoing sanctification within our hearts and minds. Be our guide and our instructor as we seek to live our lives to please you. Never quit us. I beg, Lord, no matter how we may falter, continue this blessed work you have begun. Let us truly be lights of hope in a dark world. I pray that our minds are without shadow and your pure light grows stronger by the day. For your sake and your glory, I commit myself to you. Amen.

> *When was the last time you assumed that external conformity to goodness was sufficient for pleasing God?*
> —JOSEPH M. STOWELL IN *Loving Christ*

6
Trading Places

$\mathcal{T}$ ry as she might, Melissa couldn't find a suitable pro
gram to enable her to teach beginning Spanish to her
two sons. Melissa had purchased four different resource
products but made little headway after months of concert-
ed effort. Just when Melissa was about to give up the idea
of teaching any foreign language, she heard about a newcomer to the neighborhood who was a former teacher and
a Spanish instructor no less. This lady had taken time off
from her teaching career to finish her master's degree and
was spreading the word that she was available for tutoring.
Melissa lost no time getting in touch with her. When
Melissa and Emily met they found that they had many
enthusiasms in common—not the least of which was a
mutual love for children's education and welfare. Melissa
inquired about the possibility of Emily tutoring her sons
three hours a week in basic Spanish. When Emily gave her
reply in Spanish, Melissa laughed and assumed it was
agreed.

Together, both adults set up a weekly schedule where-
upon Melissa's boys would go over to Emily's home for one
and a half hours twice weekly. In between the lessons, each
boy was given vocabulary words to memorize, a written lesson, and instructions to practice speaking any assigned

phrases to one another. When they met for lessons, Emily would look over their work, quiz them on the previously assigned material, and then present new words, phrases, and concepts. The boys loved these tutoring sessions. The sessions provided an additional challenge outside of the work Melissa gave them and they enjoyed working with another adult as well. The benefits to Melissa were positive too. She relished those hour and a half time slots when she could get her own work done without interruption. Melissa also felt a burden lift from her shoulders. With Emily as the Spanish instructor, Melissa was no longer constrained to limp along trying to teach a subject she had no skill or interest in. From every angle, hiring a tutor had worked out better than Melissa had dared hope.

For by wise guidance you will wage war
And in abundance of counselors there is victory.
—PROVERBS 24:6

Dear Lord, I am surprised at myself. I'm looking back and wondering why it has taken me so long to find the solution to this problem. You know that it has been the backdrop to so many of my thoughts of late. It seems that every avenue I tried for teaching the subject myself failed. And I did give it my best effort. But perhaps I was too determined? Was I so set on overcoming this obstacle that I didn't see that maybe I wasn't meant to teach this course? Why do I always feel that I must do everything? I hate calling upon others for help. Is this just another example of pride? I do understand that as a Christian I am part of a community. But even with my friends I have difficulty asking for assistance. I suppose that just by being a homeschooling mom I've been the brunt of skepticism so often that to admit failure is to set myself up for judgment. Lord, this is not right. I ask you to take away any fears, insecurities, or burdens that I bear. I am not able to protect myself or my family from others' critical comments. Rather, I must be willing to accept the help of those who are more skilled than I. Please let not pride hinder me from recognizing aid when it comes calling. Thank you for your good provision of a wonderfully caring tutor. I ask that you will guide her as she uses her talents to bring an added dimension to my children's educational experience. I pray that they take full advantage of this opportunity as well. Create in them a hunger for learning and give them what they need to discipline themselves for the tasks ahead. Again, Lord, I confess my unwilling heart that is frequently so resistant to help of any kind. Please forgive my stubbornness and enable me to learn from my mistakes and not repeat them in the coming days. Amen.

I am living in an all-you-can-eat restaurant, glutting on grace. I never leave the table. The banquet is forever. While I don't deserve the richness of his table, I never question its bounty.
—CALVIN MILLER IN *Jesus Loves Me*

7

Transition Alert

race was stumped. How she was ever going to squeeze in the time to help her high school age children with their advanced coursework and teach the younger ones too was beyond her reckoning. Grace never thought she'd make it so far into homeschooling to ever be facing the high school years. Many years earlier when Grace first pulled her older kids out of public school during their second and third grades, she had intended to homeschool only through elementary school. When her oldest completed the sixth grade, Grace decided to take it another year, then another, and now she had two high school students and three elementary students. Although not much daunted Grace, just looking over the prospective course work made her insides squirm. Grace was indeed a hard worker, but this seemed, well, impossible. Logistically speaking, Grace could not figure out how she would manage it all. What to do?

After perusing the many catalogs for the remainder of the afternoon, Grace sat her brood down and explained her ideas. "If this is going to work and work well, we're all going to have to pitch in with the teaching. The older ones will have to take turns fielding questions for the younger children while I trade off working with the high schoolers. It will definitely challenge our organizational skills but I think it can be done. And," Grace continued, "I've decided to look into several of the online and video courses available now. Between the two, we should cover the all the subjects required for credit later on."

Once Grace finished explaining the new system, she felt a little more at ease. Somehow, just preparing a plan always helped her overcome her nervousness. It didn't really matter that they may take an entirely different tack once school started in the fall. Grace just needed to establish a solid foundation to build on, and she was confident that any wrinkles they encountered along the way would work themselves out.

But I have received everything in full, and have an abundance; I am amply supplied.
—PHILIPPIANS 4:18

Dear Lord, this is a new road I'm embarking on now. It's a bit overwhelming to me. I've been lying awake some nights trying to map out just how to make this new school year work. With my younger children needing so much of my time and attention, I'm concerned that my oldest ones will be left floundering. You know how important it is to me that each of my children gains the best possible education. I'm now wondering if I can supply the level of instruction I long for them to experience? I'm not and never have been a gifted stu-

dent myself. What makes me think I can teach the higher-level courses? I'm not certain I can. In all honesty, I almost hoped that my children had asked to go to back into the public school system. But they didn't. They've done so well at home. Each one has achieved far beyond my expectations. I'm still in awe of the skills they've acquired and developed. Lord, I think I need another heavenly boost of confidence. I'm second-guessing my next steps, unsure what will work most efficiently. Even now, after I spent hours pouring over catalogs, looking at new materials, and talking with other home-schooling families, I'm still not 100 percent sure of what we'll be doing. Maybe that's all right. If there's one thing you've taught me, it's that flexibility is perhaps one of the most beneficial aspects of homeschooling. If we try something and it doesn't pan out, we can adjust. Thank you, Lord, for reminding me that you are the head of this family. I'm so grateful that I don't need to have all the answers today. I will make the best plans I can and you will provide the wisdom and direction to bring them to fruition. Lord, calm my heart and mind. Enable me to rest in the knowledge that you are always close by to extend assistance whenever I call. Amen.

If you can't go around it, over it, or through it, you had better negotiate with it.
—BARBARA JOHNSON IN Pack Up Your Gloomies in a Great Big Box

Rest Stops

*A*nna leaned in close and whispered to her friend Nicole, "How do keep your sanity with the kids running around the house all day?" Nicole laughed and gave Anna her trade secret.

"Once the clock strikes 2:00 P.M. everyone heads to their bedrooms for a solid hour. No exceptions."

"What if one of the kids is in the middle of an assignment and has a question?" Anna queried thoughtfully.

"He waits until 3:00 P.M. That one-hour is reserved for reading or quiet activities alone. No questions, no noise allowed."

"What if someone comes to the door or the phone rings?" Anna pressed.

"I usually turn the answering machine on and the ringer off. Although, I'd probably feel compelled to answer the door!" Nicole laughed.

"OK, you've got me convinced. Now tell me what made you decide to set up this quiet hour?"

Nicole smiled at the memory. But there was a time when Nicole wasn't so cheerful. She recalled feeling overwhelmed by the sheer busyness of her household. The constant commotion drove her nuts. The continual chattering made her head throb. Even the barrage of innocent comments and simple questions began to take their toll on Nicole's mental well-being. Finally, Nicole listened to the advice her mother had given her before her first child had even been born: "Reserve one hour every afternoon for you to replenish yourself. Make it a point to have a quiet time each day when the kids have no choice but to retreat to their rooms and you retreat to yours. Nap, exercise, read, call a friend . . . whatever you enjoy, do it." Nicole didn't take her mom's advice until she had four children under the age of six. Then on a particularly dreary day, Nicole put the youngest three down for their naps and instructed her six-year-old to look at picture books, play with her dolls, or listen to her story tapes until the kitchen buzzer sounded. Although it took a few tries before Nicole's daughter understood that mommy was serious, in time the pattern was set. Nicole frequently sends up a prayer of thanksgiving for her mother's wise counsel.

He put a new song in my mouth, a song of praise to our God.
—PSALM 40:3

Dear Lord, thank you for the sound words you gave me so many years ago. It still astounds me that I waited so long before heeding such wise advice. I remember thinking that a mom had to be pretty desperate to set aside an hour every afternoon for rest. Was I ever right! I was desperate. Desperate and despairing. Tearing my hair out and pacing in circles. My peace of mind was about shot. Lord, I can recall far too vividly just how drained I had become. I truly needed a daily respite. Still do. Nothing brings a better perspective than some solitude. Maybe it's just me, but I really do feel rejuvenated after only sixty short minutes of alone time. It doesn't always pan out, I know. Sometimes the kids come knocking on my door. Other days one of the children is sick and needs my attention. But for the most part, I believe even the children benefit from this quiet time. They seem to calm down, listen better, and even get along with their siblings more easily after resting away from the family. Lord, I cannot believe what a difference this practice has brought to us.

You alone know how I needed to regroup after spending eight or so hours caring for my children's every need. Then when schooling started, I was pulled in yet another direction. Again, I praise you for your creative provision. You always stand ready to usher in newfound hope and renewed purpose. Never leave me alone to face the responsibilities that mothering brings. Lord, teach me how to draw my strength from the reservoir of your goodness each day. Let me pass on your legacy of love to my children as well. Amen.

The bow cannot always be bent without fear of breaking. For a field to bear fruit, it must occasionally lie fallow. And for you to be healthy, you must rest. Slow down, and God will heal you.
—MAX LUCADO IN *Traveling Light for Mothers*

9

Under the Weather

Rejoicing that her only child would soon have a sibling, Lindsay sat down and wept tears of jubilation. Lindsay and her husband of ten years had had no trouble conceiving their daughter Jackie some eight years ago. But after hoping and praying for another baby since the birth of their first, Lindsay was ecstatic. Together, their small family rejoiced and thanked God that another little one was on its way.

Lindsay's enthusiasm didn't last long, however. Mere days after she learned she was pregnant, Lindsay became so ill that she couldn't handle any food. Every time Lindsay tried to eat even the smallest meal, what she got down came right back up. Little enough nutrition was making it into her system, and even holding down liquids became difficult. Worried that her baby wasn't receiving what it needed to develop and grow properly, Lindsay kept in close contact with her doctor. After weeks of losing not only food but her strength, Lindsay was hospitalized for dehydration. During the three days she was in the hospital, Lindsay found herself on the receiving end of too much advice. "Send Jackie to school for the rest of the school year," her advisers chimed in. "You'll be able to regain your strength faster. Give yourself time to recover and prepare for the new baby.

Next year, you can bring Jackie home again to homeschool. Surely, one semester won't make any difference," they claimed.

"But it will make a huge difference to me!" Lindsay cried. Frazzled and forlorn, Lindsay didn't have it in her to fight against so many voices of reason. She simply didn't have the strength to resist. So Lindsay called in the troops. Before Lindsay left the hospital, her friends had already set up a visitation schedule whereby one of the twelve moms in Lindsay's homeschooling group would take turns overseeing Jackie's work for a given day. Sometime in the late afternoon, the mom on call would deliver a simple meal, check over Jackie's assignments and do a quick clean-up chore at Lindsay's house. Since Lindsay's morning sickness wouldn't last forever (she hoped), these faithful friends figured they could afford to volunteer a few hours of their time for such a worthwhile cause.

Beloved, I pray that in all respects you may prosper and be in good health, just as your soul prospers.
—3 JOHN 2

Dear Lord, how can I express my gratitude? You have given me not one, but many marvelous gifts. I am so very humbled by your goodness to me. Thank you for bringing such blessing into our lives. We have waited so long for this day to arrive. You know it well. I have prayed for such a day for many, many years. And in the midst of such joy, I have found to my delight and wonder just how dedicated my dear friends are to me and my family. All of these women are already so busy with their own families. Still, they are taking time to minister to mine. How can I ever repay their goodness? In truth, they epitomize the Proverbs 31 woman who rises early and sees to the needs of others. I am in awe of their generosity and love. As I seek to strengthen my body, help me be wise. I know that in my impatience to get back on my feet, I might be tempted to take on more than I should. Lord, you alone know how many days I must rest. Help me resist the temptation to push too hard, too fast. I pray that you bring healing and renewed vigor back to my body even now. But I'm also learning many sweet lessons by staying quiet and still as my body recovers. Please continue to protect my unborn child as it grows within me. Watch over its soul, and give this little one whatever is needed to develop. I thank you again for surrounding me with people who love us enough to sacrifice themselves on our behalf. You are a mighty God and I praise you. Amen.

As we exercise the positive, the negative diminishes in strength.
—JIM DOWLING IN *Meditation: The Bible Tells You How*

10

No Rest for the Weary

*I*mmediately after church services on Sunday, Rhonda changed into some comfortable clothes and started cooking dinner. Although Rhonda had had the foresight to prepare a large pan of lasagna and a salad on Saturday to make for a more restful Sunday, she had neglected to set aside the remainder of the day for the same purpose. Instead, while dinner was cooking, Rhonda dashed downstairs and put a load of clothes into the washer, unloaded the dishwasher, and looked over the bills that needed paying. She continued working around the house tidying this and that until the kitchen timer sounded. At the table, Rhonda felt pleased with what she already had accomplished. Mentally, she continued tabulating a few more tasks she could complete after she finished cleaning up the kitchen. If I can get to the ironing and finish up all the clothes, Monday morning will certainly easier to take. I may even be able to strip the bedding today too if I keep the washer going constantly. Hmm . . . what else can I do today?

Rhonda did exactly as she planned. In fact, she was so industrious that she not only completed the items on her to-do list but she also squeezed in a few extras before bedtime. But come Monday morning Rhonda could hardly get out of bed. By midday, she was really dragging. "I need a nap, kids." Off to her room she went for a ten-minute rest.

When Rhonda awoke over an hour later she was still groggy and tired. What's with me today? Then it hit her. What irony! Everything Rhonda worked so hard to get done on Sunday had caught up with her on Monday. She realized that even she needed a day off from work. Be it housework or homework, everyone functions better after having taken a day in the week to rest. Lord help me to remember how awful I feel right now the next time I have the urge to use Sundays as a way to "get ahead" of the game.

"Remember the sabbath day, to keep it holy. Six days you shall labor and do all your work."
—EXODUS 20:8–9

Dear Lord, it's me again, coming back to say I'm so determined to do things my way that I end up paying the price many times over for not listening to you. I'm thinking about why I am so stubborn, Lord. What makes me think I know better how to govern my life than you, my creator? Time and time again, I refuse to adhere to your wise counsel. I know I need rest. I certainly don't believe I have a boundless supply of energy. Today proved that. Still, even in the face of such knowledge, I go my own way. I wear myself out trying to stay on task. More foolishly, I sacrifice the one day you have set aside for rest and I choose to work. Somehow, I convince myself that if I get Monday's work done on Sunday then I'll feel less pressure during the upcoming week. That makes little sense, I know.

Lord, can you help me work through these compulsions I harbor that drive me to work until I drop? I cannot imagine a day without some kind of labor! Isn't that tragic? I am not some invincible woman. When I try to do too much, my family suffers as well. I'm not able to teach my kids with the energy and enthusiasm they deserve. I cannot even think straight without taking some time off to rest and rejuvenate. I hope that this is the last time I'll come whining about my lack of discipline. For truly, if I cannot stop myself from working, then I'm no more in control than the person who refuses to work at all. Lord, I am of the mind that moderation is the key. Will you continue to work with me that I might achieve this delicate balance in all areas? There is nothing I can accomplish that will cause your love for me to increase or diminish. I do cling to this truth. Amen.

He loves me in spite of the fact that I can do nothing for him. He loves me because he cannot help himself. I love him because I am helpless without his love.
—CALVIN MILLER IN *Jesus Loves Me*

Have Books, Will Travel

Ashley received the news with little comment. She never complained. It would only make her husband feel worse. But what didn't show on the outside churned deep within Ashley's heart. It was another move for their family. The fourth in as many years. Ashley hated having to tell the children they would be leaving again. Their son and daughter would balk, of course. Who wouldn't? But every time they moved, Ashley secretly harbored the dim hope that maybe this would be last time. It wasn't so much for her sake as for the children's. It was tough being pulled out of one school and placed in another, friendless. Ashley sympathized with her two youngsters. Though she always put on a brave face for them, everyone felt the same way. Mentally, Ashley began listing the obstacles she'd have to face yet a fourth time. Crushed under the weight of it all, Ashley called her sister with the news. Twenty minutes later, Ashley's countenance wasn't so defeated. Two hours later, Ashley fairly beamed. We'll try it, she said with conviction, it can't be any harder than what we've already faced.

During that twenty-minute conversation with her sister, Ashley was introduced to the idea of homeschooling.

Instead of offering trite solutions to Ashley's dilemma, her sister suggested they try schooling the children at home. "This way," she commented, "both kids can stay current with their studies before, during, and after the move. They won't have to jump into another system's curriculum midyear. Nor will they have to adjust to a whole new routine all at once. With homeschooling, they'll at least have daily continuity, and it may make the transition to another city easier on them." And on me, thought Ashley. This just may be the best solution yet.

And not only this, but we also exult in our tribulations, knowing that tribulation brings about perseverance; and perseverance, proven character; and proven character, hope; and hope does not disappoint, because the love of God has been poured out within our hearts through the Holy Spirit who was given to us.
—ROMANS 5:3–5

Dear Lord, I am wearied just thinking about all the changes our family will soon have to endure. This is not the lifestyle I had envisioned for us and I do get concerned for our children. Constant changes are often so hard on them. As their mom, I ache inside when I think of them having to say more goodbyes. Lord, I know I have to accept this change. I need you to give me your grace to get through it another time. But I have a renewed hope. One less burden to bear. We are going to attempt schooling our children at home. As soon as I heard the idea suggested, something inside me leaped. I really believe this may be just the avenue we need to overcome some of the stresses of moving. Lord, I've never thought of myself as a teacher. Some might think me crazy for taking on such a responsibility and moving, too. But, I'm confident that although this change will be different, it will also alleviate many of my own personal concerns for my children. Thank you, Lord. You have provided the answer to our problem. Even now, I am beginning to sense that inner excitement grow. In the midst of all the changes, I simply ask that you hold us tight, keep up close to your heart, and give us what we require to transform a tense time into the smoothest transition yet. Show yourself strong on our behalf as you always do. Amen.

Faith is not some weak and pitiful emotion, but is strong and vigorous confidence built on the fact that God is holy love. And even though you cannot see Him right now and cannot understand what He is doing, you know Him.
—OSWALD CHAMBERS IN *My Utmost for His Highest*

PART TWO

Teaching Day by Day

Some moms seem to find their stride from day one and never look back. For most mothers, however, learning how to manage the educational responsibilities and teach one's children with confidence takes time. Setbacks, trial and error, and discouragement are all part and parcel of discovering how your family will function most efficiently. Determine to set reasonable goals and strive to accomplish them as consistently as possible. Incremental progress, day by day, will yield amazing results over time. Give yourself room to grow into the role of a teaching mom and you'll be surprised how adept you become as the months go by.

12

Lend a Hand

$\mathcal{E}$very Tuesday morning after breakfast, Jodi and her brood of four children check the list that is displayed on the front of their refrigerator. This chore sheet divides the housecleaning tasks into five separate categories. Jodi assigns each child one area for an entire month and she takes on the fifth and most difficult cleaning job: the bathrooms and the floors. Friends often ask in wonder how Jodi manages to keep a clean and well-organized house even while homeschooling. Jodi shrugs and casually comments that her kids are a big help. In fact, so automatically ingrained is this pattern of pitching in and getting the work done first, that Jodi hardly thinks about it anymore. It isn't until a friend calls and complains that her house is a mess or that she just can't keep up with laundry, dishes, and school, let alone the house, that Jodi realizes how blessed she is.

But it wasn't always that way. Jodi still remembers when her four children were all under the age of six. Those early days of motherhood were exhausting. She literally did not sit down all day except to feed the children at meal times. Even then, Jodi was up and about throughout breakfast, lunch, and dinner; wiping up spills, refilling drinks, washing sticky fingers and faces. Then came cleanup, with one child hanging on her leg and a baby strapped into his portable chair, Jodi would bounce with one foot and maintain balance with the other, all while doing the dishes. Those early years were a blur to Jodi. But Jodi also remembers the day her husband suggested that she enlist the older two children in simple chores. Although it took a while to teach them to properly sweep the floors or dust the furniture, eventually Jodi's children became skilled at both light and deep cleaning the entire house. They didn't always accomplish the job in the same way Jodi might have desired, but once the learning curve was complete, each child became adept in a variety of skills. Admittedly, it took time for Jodi to teach her children these tasks, but Jodi has realized the benefit of this investment for years, and her kids now fully appreciate all that it requires to manage a household of six people.

Walk in a manner worthy of the Lord, to please Him in all respects, bearing fruit in every good work and increasing in the knowledge of God.
—COLOSSIANS 1:10

Dear Lord, I pray that my children come to understand that work is a gift. I want them to fully grasp that any labor that is done with diligence and skill is a blessing. Help them realize that it does not matter what task we set our hands to accomplish; it only matters that we do it with all our strength. My hope for my children is that they learn to exercise their will to do what is right, not what is merely expedi-

ent. *Please do not allow them to give in to laziness or selfishness. Help me be a constant example in this area.*

Lord, I recognize that as I instruct my children in the areas of work and responsibility, I am equipping them to serve you. I do them no favor when I release them from their tasks for little reason. Yet there are times when I would gladly do their work as well as my own to save myself from their grumbling. I recognize that this, too, is just one part of the process. At each step in the training, I must not shirk my duty to teach them right responses and entreat them to think through their attitudes. Help me stay the course, Lord. And when I begin to lose patience, give me the grace I require to speak with a gentle calmness. Let me demonstrate my willingness to serve you, Lord, in the way I choose to become a servant to my family. Amen.

> *True service is a lifestyle. It acts from ingrained patterns of living. It springs spontaneously to meet human need.*
> —RICHARD J. FOSTER IN *Celebration of Discipline*

13

A Purposeful Pace

Thirty-seven-year-old Amy, mom to two boys and formerly an airline stewardess, understood the meaning of managing time. Amy had traveled the world for over nine years before making the decision to have children and stay home with her family. During Amy's flying years, she set a grueling pace. Amy always signed on for the overseas trips and reveled in staying at the task for as many consecutive flights allowed by her airline. Energetic and goal-oriented, Amy never lacked for opportunities to serve others on countless excursions around the world. In fact, although it had been Amy's decision to start a family, her husband, Matt, wondered whether Amy would miss all the excitement. But she didn't. Once Amy's son was born, Amy understood she was trading one active and exciting lifestyle for another.

Certainly, life was different now. Amy's entire world centered around her home instead of circling the globe. But everything she loved was now within this small segment of the world as well. Before Amy had even fully adjusted to parenting one child, she became pregnant with the second. Within eighteen months, Amy was mother to two young boys. Those first few years flew by, and Amy relished her sons' every milestone as they grew and developed. By the time the school years came around, Amy and Matt opted for homeschooling. Kindergarten was noneventful. Even first and second grades went well. But once Amy had been home educating both her sons for about two years, she started to feel the pressure of having to handle the multitude of responsibilities. Days flew by and Amy would realize she hadn't accomplished nearly the amount of work she'd hoped. She grew frustrated as she tried to play "catch-up" on the weekends once her husband was home. Instead, the weekends only brought extra activities and pressures. Amy, once renowned for her indomitable spirit, was discouraged and depressed. Her husband grew concerned. Amy herself couldn't understand her own emotions, which frightened her as well. *I need to take some time,* Amy considered, *to reevaluate my priorities. I really must schedule in some "alone time" to just think and pray every day, otherwise I'll never get beyond the rush-rush and embrace what my life has to offer.*

O God, Thou art my God; I shall seek Thee earnestly;
My soul thirsts for Thee, my flesh yearns for Thee,
In a dry and weary land where there is no water.
—PSALM 63:1

Dear Lord, I'd like to tell you how I'm feeling today. But I don't know that I'm able to express in words all that I'm experiencing within my heart. It's frightening to feel so despondent, so discouraged. Perhaps even more scary is that I have no concrete reasons for how I feel. Looking from the outside, I have a life many would gladly trade for. Yet I feel lost amidst all the busyness. Every choice I make seems to converge with another, and the mere number of options is overwhelming me. This is so unlike me. I used to thrive on accomplishment and challenge. Not anymore. Maybe it's because I don't see the point in many of the "good things" people are compelling me to take part in. I pray that you shine your light bright into my soul and help me find release for this anguish. I am like a lost sheep. I don't have the strength or the wisdom to make the decisions I need to make. Lord, I am afraid. My family is counting on me as they always have. So I must now count upon you. Let your goodness envelop me. Release a generous portion of your joy and peace into my heart. Help me not be overcome by the unknown future but to take stock of today and live my utmost for the time given me. Please reach down and minister to me in my confusion. Set my heart upon the right path and walk this road with me. Amen.

> *All around us there are clues that God is at work answering prayer, sparing us from something unpleasant or dangerous, teaching us something about Himself. Divine pennies gleam at our feet. How often do we step on them or ignore them in the busyness of life?*
> —ANN KROEKER IN *The Contemplative Mom*

Making Up the Difference

A quick backward glance toward the kitchen clock told Lisa all she needed to know. They were behind, again. There never seemed to be enough time to complete each lesson in an orderly fashion. One child would finish his math assignment while Lisa read to her second child in another room, then they'd switch places. Of course, there was always some overlap when the child working mathematics problems had questions and Lisa would stop her reading to assist him. After reading assignments and math lessons were done, it was general language arts, which combined spelling, creative writing, and grammar work. Next came alternative days of science and health labs, with history following. At last, lunch break arrived with an extra half hour of "free time" tossed in to preserve Lisa's sanity. At 1:00 P.M., it was back into the school mode for computer work and art or foreign language study. By 2:30 P.M., Lisa was spent. On those rare days when her children did manage to stay on schedule, Lisa rejoiced. But there were far too many afternoons that Lisa kicked herself for not accomplishing everything she'd set out to do for the day.

Lisa struggled with significant self-doubts regarding her capacity as her children's teacher. She wasn't confident that she had the skills necessary to teach her children adequately. It unnerved Lisa when she overheard other moms casually chatting about their latest milestones as home instructors to their junior high and high school teens. *I'll never be able to handle those upper grades,* Lisa worried. What Lisa didn't yet understand is that her homeschooling style would grow and change right along with her children's ages and abilities. In fact, Lisa herself would do the orchestrating and making of subtle changes as she became more comfortable with the whole homeschooling arena. At this point, Lisa only needed to do one thing. Relax.

"Come to Me, all who are weary and heavy-laden, and I will give you rest. Take My yoke upon you, and learn from Me, for I am gentle and humble in heart; and you shall find rest for your souls. For My yoke is easy, and My load is light."
—MATTHEW 11:28–30

Dear Lord, another day to tackle what's before me and I'm already uptight. I'm so high-strung and anxious about this homeschooling that I never seem to relax anymore. Lord, I believe that we have made a good and right choice to educate our children in our home. Why is it, then, that I am so nervous? I want some assurances that I'm covering all the bases with them. I most definitely have my weak areas and I feel compelled to see that my kids don't suffer because of my lack.

I suppose what I really am searching for is a foolproof guarantee that nothing will go amiss while I'm the one in charge. I know this is not possible. All of life is rife with uncertainties; I'd simply like to believe otherwise. Lord, meet me at my weakest point and renew my frail heart. I'm standing in your presence awaiting your grace and strength to give me what I require for today's needs. Let me stand strong in your strength. Give me all the wisdom and insight I require to teach my children in your ways. Let them see in me a mother who has the stamina and fortitude to press ahead despite setbacks and discouragement. I must thank you for allowing me to understand perhaps the most significant truth I'll ever glean. My weakness invites your strength. Show yourself strong in my life, Lord. Let your resilient love pour forth from me as I work to serve my family in this way. I am your child and I am so very grateful that you, as my father, are constantly standing at the ready to meet my every need. I am in awe of you, Lord. I pray that today I show evidence of my trust in you. Amen.

That's the hook we hang our hope on, sisters. Not in "getting it right," but in knowing that although we get it wrong—over and over, consistently, even blatantly—God's power to accomplish his will is not limited to our meager efforts.
—LIZ CURTIS HIGGS IN *Really Bad Girls of the Bible*

15

A Peaceful Proposal

A veteran homeschooling mom, Patty was mother to six children and had homeschooled her entire brood for over thirteen years. Patty, as mothers of large families are wont to be, was extremely organized. Everything she did was preplanned and frequently written on a to-do list she posted on her refrigerator door. Even Patty's children knew the routine by heart. Each morning it was do the chores, eat breakfast, clean their bedrooms, read the Bible and pray, then hit the books all by 9:00 A.M. Patty believed with all her heart that a clean, well-run home was not only conducive to a good learning environment, it was essential. And Patty's efforts were obviously paying off. Her children were a delight and their study system had proved successful, too, since all their tests came back with glowing results.

But Patty's friend Chris was often upset at Patty's "school at home" approach to teaching. Chris was at the opposite end of the homeschooling spectrum: she fervently believed that children would learn all they need to know as they experienced life on a day-to-day basis. She was the poster mom for the "unschooling" movement. Chris allowed her children freedom to pick up a book at their leisure and work their math problems when it interested them; she relied heavily on "life experiences" such as cooking, gardening, and animal husbandry to teach her kids basic skills.

The only schooling issue Patty and Chris really agreed upon was how valuable their monthly field trips were to rounding out the children's education. On that, they did concur. Still, their friendship was strained, and both women were bent on convincing the other she was mistaken. Other moms within their group looked on in amazement and despair. Finally, after months of witnessing Patty and Chris debate each other, one of the newest moms to the group challenged them, "Why does it matter how you homeschool your kids as long as you're getting the job done?" Patty looked at Chris. Chris looked at Patty. "Ouch," the expressions on their faces said what words wouldn't.

"Do not judge lest you be judged. For in the way you judge, you will be judged; and by your standard of measure, it will be measured to you."
—MATTHEW 7:1–2

Dear Lord, another conversation with my friend turned ugly. I am ashamed to say that we don't agree on much and we've allowed our differences to cloud our friendship. I never thought that others would notice the fact that we disagreed. But it has happened and this is another reason for a closer look at inner motives. Why do I feel so compelled to have my opinion accepted? What is it in me that cannot stand for someone to disagree? I realize that we both feel strongly about homeschooling. Both of us are moms who are committed to providing our children with the best education possible. So why do we sit on divergent sides of this issue? Truthfully, I cannot see how my friend has arrived at her stance. But she believes she is honoring you through her choices. She is confident that her mode of teaching is the best for her children. Then who am I to question? Lord, please intercede in this situation. It has become such a sore point between the two of us. Now others have entered the fray as well. This is not good. I admit to having set myself up as both judge and jury over my friend. Please forgive me. Give me the grace to ask her forgiveness as well. And help me maintain a quiet, gentle spirit when we next meet. Shower me with your generous provision of grace and enable me to resist voicing my own opinion. I want our group to be united. We won't always be in agreement on specifics, but we can surely stand together as homeschoolers. Lord, give us your wisdom and let your lavish grace permeate our conversation from this day forward. Amen.

Your attitude to your fellow-men, good and bad, nice and nasty, both Christians and unbelievers, is to be that of the Good Samaritan towards the Jew in the gutter—that is to say, your eyes must be open to see others' needs both spiritual and material.
—J. I. PACKER IN *Knowing God*

16
Ordering My Day

The clothes and bedding were washed, dried, folded, and put away. The ironing was completed. The bills had been paid, and dinner was already simmering in the Crock-Pot for the evening's meal. Jeannie felt pleased that she'd accomplished so much and all before lunch, too. In fact, Jeannie had already checked off everything she'd needed to do for the day. Everything, that is, except school her children. Jeannie grimaced. Well, they have gotten their math and reading assignments done. Or have they? Jeannie handed out the day's school work each morning first thing after breakfast, and her kids knew what they were expected to complete. Generally, Jeannie's children sat at the kitchen table and quietly did their assignments while Jeannie looked on and took turns helping them or taking one child into another room for a separate lesson. This system was working so well that Jeannie began taking advantage of those snatches of time when all her kids were immersed in their work to tackle some of her own chores.

Jeannie had always marveled at the other home-schooling moms, who told her to multi-task otherwise she'd never get everything accomplished. So, in her own way, Jeannie was learning to multitask. The only problem was that now instead of simply taking the opportunities to complete her responsibilities while the children were otherwise occupied, Jeannie inadvertently began making her work top priority. She loved the feeling of having done all her tasks for the day by lunchtime. Before long, Jeannie's work came first and the children's school assignments were being squeezed in around her own to-do list. What started out as a great system quickly turned sour. Jeannie would get impatient when her kids interrupted her before she was finished. Her children would get frustrated that Mom wasn't available to answer questions and offer guidance when they needed it. After a few months of trial and error, Jeannie realized that every day was a busy day. She'd just need to prioritize better and put the children's schooling at the top of the list once and for all.

For every house is built by someone, but the builder of all things is God.
—Hebrews 3:4

Dear Lord, I've been trying to figure out a way to accomplish everything I need to do by day's end. I thought that I could finish up all my responsibilities and still have plenty of time left for school. Perhaps I may eventually reach this goal. But right now, I'm just getting the hang of this homeschooling world, and trying to maintain my home on top of it just about does me in. Our home was always so orderly and organized. I never felt so pressured by time before. Somehow, even with all the little ones, I managed to stay current. Now with schooling it's a whole new world. I just cannot seem to keep pace with my kids' educational needs and the myriad household tasks, too. I'm thinking that more than any "plan" I need a new perspective. In the back of my mind, I can hear the same refrain playing over and over. I must put the children's schooling first. I need to allow for some unfinished work around the house. Flexibility is the key word here. Lord, give me what I require to let go of some of my perfectionist standards. I will never be able to regain this day once it is over. Time will race by and my children won't necessarily remember a sparkling home. What they will recall is that their mom took time for them, listened to them, and loved them. I can't say this transition is going to be easy, but I'm willing to try. I never want to emulate Martha's busyness at the expense of Mary's devotion. Again, Lord, meet me at my place of need. Renew my heart for the things of God and set my priorities in their proper place. Be pleased to take over as the master builder of my home. Amen.

We all want shortcuts—to happiness, to success, to health, to everything of value. Most shortcuts do not work. They lead to disappointment and disaster, disillusionment and failure. For the things in life that count the most, there are no lottery winners, no instant riches, no immediate happiness.
—JERRY WHITE IN Making Peace with Reality

17
Crunch Time

ina placed the last of the lunch fixings into the brown paper bags. Her husband's and daughters' lunches were all ready to go and Tina looked around the kitchen for a moment. Mentally, she was tabulating what quick chores she could finish before heading to their home office for an hour or so of work. While her high school age daughters raced around gathering their books, lunches, and backpacks, Tina stood off to the side and wished them all a good day before waving them off. After breathing a quick, silent prayer for her husband and daughters, Tina headed into the office for what she considered her one window of opportunity in the day to get some much-needed business accomplished. Occasionally, Tina looked at the minuscule digital clock on her computer as she busily typed away the precious minutes. Before she knew it, Tina could hear the footfalls on the floor above her head. Her youngest two children were now up and around. Since they both had about a half an hour's worth of daily morning chores, which included feeding and watering the outside animals, cleaning up their bedrooms, and dressing, Tina sighed as she the clock kept ticking. A few more minutes and I'll be done, she thought satisfied.

When the back door banged shut and opened again, water ran, and footsteps clumped inside again, Tina knew it was time to go back upstairs and begin her day a second time. With two elementary age children still being home-schooled, Tina frequently felt like she was straddling two worlds. Her oldest children now attended a public high school, which necessitated parental involvement on a variety of fronts. Yet her daytime hours were spent schooling her youngest two at home. Tina could now understand how mothers with children at both ends of the age spectrum felt because she was being pulled from every angle. Some days, it was all Tina could do to simply keep pace with her family's ever expanding and bustling schedule.

For we are His workmanship, created in Christ Jesus for good works, which God prepared beforehand, that we should walk in them.
—EPHESIANS 2:10

Dear Lord, it's another day, another call to get up and moving early on so I don't fall behind in my work. I admit to feeling a deep-seated weariness when I even contemplate the upcoming week. My guess had been that it would have gotten much easier for me with my oldest children now in school. In some ways, I suppose it has lightened my load. It's amazing that I was ever able to keep up with each child's workload. Still, though I'm juggling fewer subject areas, I'm now wearing the hats of both homeschool mom and public school mom. I feel like I'm living in a perpetual crunch-time mode. If I get even slightly off-track with our daily schedule it's mighty hard to get back on. Lord, there must be some trick to handling these busy, stressful seasons. Perhaps it's just my attitude that needs adjusting? Maybe there isn't any organizational change we need to make. I'm getting this feeling that my life, our family's life, will be always be fraught with demands on our time. Our resources will run low, we will face urgent requests, and our patience levels will wane. Lord, show us how to live according to your ways. Help us make those ruthless decisions that guard our family's time against frivolous and wasteful pursuits. Give us the wisdom we need to say no to anything that will separate us from your highest calling in our lives. In truth, we have too many choices, far too many opportunities. Let us choose wisely in all areas. And enable me, Lord, to disengage from the day's demands and seek out solitary moments of refreshment with you. Draw me ever closer to your heart. Make me into a woman of quietness and let serenity guard my heart at all times. Finally, I pray that all our work be acceptable in your sight. Amen.

Kairos moments are never pragmatic moves to ensure a blessed life during our short tenure on earth. They are moments to be seized for the sake of eternity and for the Lord of eternity.
—JAMES EMERY WHITE IN *Life-Defining Moments*

18
Lift Up Your Eyes

*C*hecking her daily calendar against her daughter's soccer practices and games, Erin almost cried. With these new fall sports beginning practices earlier into the summer every year, it seemed to whittle down what little free time her family had left. With soccer looming large, piano lessons on Fridays, Pioneer Girls meeting on Thursdays, youth group gatherings on Sunday evenings, and biweekly homeschooling meetings to boot, there were very few open spaces left on the calendar. Not to forget family commitments, birthdays, other church service responsibilities either. Erin prayed no one got sick—they wouldn't have time to be ill. Pathetic, Erin muttered to herself. How many times did I hear myself say, "Our family absolutely will not fall into the over-commitment trap?" But here we are.

Unlike some parents, Erin wasn't harboring some inner fear that her kids would miss out if they didn't participate in a multitude of extracurricular activities. She knew both her children were well-adjusted, happy kids. So how did this barrage of "extras" creep into their lives? Erin already knew the answer. She remembered getting a call from one friend, then another, who would ask Erin if her children would like to participate in such and such. They did, of course, and Erin wanted to provide some outside interests for her children. Eventually, one too many affirmative replies had snowballed into a nightmarish life of running her kids places every day of the week save one. Erin took her pen and calendar in hand for a second time. She continued filling in the days for all their various activities. Then she did something courageous. Erin began blocking out two nights every week for the remainder of the school year. These days are sacred family times, Erin told herself. When someone calls and asks me to join another club, serve on another committee, I can honestly tell them we already have something on the calendar.

> *For our citizenship is in heaven, from which also we eagerly wait for a Savior, the Lord Jesus Christ.*
> —PHILIPPIANS 3:20

Dear Lord, I'd like to come before your throne with nothing in my heart but thanksgiving and praise. But I've gotten our family into such a mess that until I pray this through, I don't think I can concentrate on anything else. I remember, when my children were small, that I told others that I would not fall into the busyness trap. I could see how being overcommitted was tearing apart families all around me. They never had time for one another, didn't know each other because they were all running in different directions. It grieved me to see how distant these families became. And their children harbored so much stress for ones so young. Yet now I find myself falling into the same pattern. Somehow I've said yes too many times. I didn't mean for this to happen. But it has, and now my family is experiencing all the burnout I've observed in others. Lord, help me set a more reasonable pace. I truly believe I've allowed myself to be content with what this world can offer us. What has happened to our hope for heaven? Have we lost our eagerness to live this life in preparation for the next? Do I even consider how my choices today will affect my citizenship in heaven? I'm ashamed to admit that it rarely crosses my mind. From this perspective, does one more class really make that much difference? Will mastering two musical instruments really benefit my children's character? What has happened to the balance I so strove for? Lord, I cannot turn back the clock, but I can make better choices in the days to come. I ask for your insight to wisely choose. Help me discern between the good and the best. Let every decision I make be tempered by thoughts of eternity. Hold me accountable for how I manage my time and that of my family. Lord, I know you can redeem the lost hours and I ask that you begin even this moment. Amen.

> *It is an affront and embarrassment to Him when we become so earthly-minded, so consumed by wanting what the world has, so embittered over what it doesn't, so troubled by our circumstances, that we give no thought to what He has prepared for us.*
> —MARK BUCHANAN IN *Things Unseen*

19

Give It a Whirl

G iving the globe a last spin, Judy felt discouraged. "Put your books and maps away, kids. Carefully." As a former travel agent, Judy had traveled the world before marrying and having children. Though years had passed, Judy would occasionally reminisce about those colorful, fast-paced days. On those days she would drag out her photo albums and show her children more about the trips she had taken. No doubt about it, geography was the subject she liked to teach best. With contacts all around the country, Judy still received exciting information about new travel opportunities. But Judy no longer felt that old thrill of adventure when she perused the enticing flyers. Rather, she experienced an increased sense of frustration. Heatedly, Judy carried on a regular mental debate with herself. She rehashed the same ground time after time. Sure, she thought, I gave up working to be home with my kids, no regrets there. But without my second income, we don't have the money to take our kids to any of these fascinating places. There's so much I want my family to experience with me. I have so many ideas, so little hope of ever seeing them come true. Just how do I bring these geographical wonders to life for my kids? Nothing can compare with being there, or can it?

Out of desperation, Judy thought of a way to bring a bit of her old world into her children's. She decided upon a destination and together they planned the trip. Judy had the children study everything pertinent to their vicarious destination. They learned about the people, their cultural history, the climate, the food and traditions, religious practices, everything and anything to make the country come alive. Then they planned where they would stay, what interesting sites they would visit. As they made notes as they went along, Judy's children became more and more enthused. Finally, after exhausting all avenues for discovering information, Judy took it upon herself to prepare a wrap-up presentation. She cooked a culturally appropriate feast, they played games, and Judy even found a movie for the children to enjoy centered around their location. Although it wasn't as good as actually visiting in person, Judy deemed the venture a success when her kids clamored to start another study right away.

───

Not that I speak from want; for I have learned to be content in whatever circumstances I am.
—PHILIPPIANS 4:11

Dear Lord, I have to confess that I've been fussing again. Please forgive me for being so shortsighted. I seem to be in a constant state of "want." Lord, I know this attitude is not good. It destroys all the joy within my heart. I believe I need to better grasp that life doesn't merely exist for the taking.

When we decided to school our children in the home, we knew it would require a financial sacrifice. I suppose I didn't realize how large and all-encompassing that sacrifice would be. Maybe I just didn't want to think about all the missed opportunities I might have to accept. But you know my heart, Lord. I have not accepted any cutbacks with good grace. I may not voice my frustrations out loud, but my heart bucks against each and every one. I cry unfair all too often. I suppose I think someone should be paying me back for all my hard work within my home. I know this is unreasonable. Still, I can't seem to work through my discontent. I need your touch again, Lord. I really want to rest in this place you have me in. And, truth be told, I love being home with my children. I wouldn't trade this time with them for any amount of money. Still, my mother's heart wants to give to them. I desire for them to experience all the good things this world has to offer. Perhaps I'm not focusing on what is truly of worth? Lord, I cannot trust in my emotions, that much is certain. I am in need of your wisdom to clear my mind of unproductive thoughts and wrong desires. Purify me with your heavenly light. Give me a renewed sense of purpose. Remake me as I continue to come before your throne in petition and prayer. Amen.

There are burdens that can be borne only in prayer.
—Evelyn Christenson in *Lord, Change Me*

PART THREE

Character Development

Perhaps some of the most meaningful and lasting lessons children learn are not those tied to academic instruction. The development of character qualities such as diligence, strong work ethic, patience, kindness, selflessness, and determination will be lessons learned throughout the day and within the framework of a variety of situations. As the teaching mom prepares for her school day, she recognizes that her children's attitudes (as well as her own) can serve to build up or tear down the very fabric of family life. Viewing home education as an opportunity to influence young hearts and minds for eternity is indeed a high calling and privilege.

20

Time Out!

*L*istening to the clamoring going on between her children in the next room, Sheri felt like joining in by clashing and banging the two pans she held in her hands. As she tried to maintain a sense of calm, Sheri pushed away the temptation to release her mounting frustration via the frying pans and instead strode purposefully into the living room. "That's it," Sheri said loudly enough to be heard over the din of sibling disputes. "Each of you, into your own room, now. March," Sheri instructed. It must have been something in her voice that urged Sheri's three children to obey without complaint. They could tell better than Sheri herself when it was time to listen with no further comment. This afternoon was plainly one of those occasions.

Sheri had fielded telephone calls for her family all day, schooled the children until 2:00 P.M., even made a fast dash for a few groceries she'd needed for tonight's dinner. Then, when Sheri thought she could relax for a moment, another telephone call came that dashed her spirits. A good friend's teenage son had again turned to violence in a fit of rage. Sheri's friend, in tears, had called the police, who in turn had taken the boy to an underage holding facility in the city. Devastated, Sheri tried to console her friend. Sheri promised her that she would be over as soon as her husband arrived home from work. Sheri hung up the phone and tried to pray for her friend. But then she was interrupted by her own children's cries of anger. Something snapped inside Sheri. She knew that no family was immune to the dangers of uncontrolled emotions. It was time again to appeal to her kids' hearts and not simply administer a discipline they'd soon forget. Sheri felt desperate to impart lasting truth to her family; she never wanted to be the one making the telephone call she'd just received.

This you know, my beloved brethren. But let everyone be quick to hear, slow to speak and slow to anger; for the anger of man does not achieve the righteousness of God.
—JAMES 1:19–20

Dear Lord, at this moment, I feel so overwhelmed with my own emotions that I could easily vent toward my own family. I am saddened by my friend's situation. It troubles me deeply that her once loving child has turned on her. She is grieving beyond measure, Lord. I pray that you'll be with her, hold her fast. Give her all that she requires at this time to continue mothering her other children with steadfastness and courage. I commit this tragedy into your so capable hands and ask that you embrace my friend. Draw her loved one back to you as well. Speak to the heart and reach into the depths of each soul. Show each one how great your love is for them even now. Let them understand that forgiveness is always available; that healing is ever at the heart's door awaiting an invitation.

And Lord, I am troubled over my own family. I sense a building tide of anger within the hearts of my children. I see their selfish natures vie for preeminence. Worst of all, I see them mirror my own heart. I, too, must confess that I am frequently angry. I give voice to my own "rights" far too often. Lord, please forgive me. Help me overcome this bent I have embraced for so long. Let me recognize that I am to focus on serving those around me for your sake. I know that as I let go of expectations, you reward me with blessings beyond any of my own making. You are my treasure, my communion with you, Lord, is what my heart yearns for. Open my understanding and show me how to be an example of quietness and peace to my children. Give us your wisdom as we work through difficult times within our own family. Impart to us your principles of life, which will bring healing and restoration among us. Amen.

> *You [parents] must be willing to lay aside your personal rights and forgive your child's offense against you so that you may focus on fulfilling your parental obligations to him.*
> —Lou Priolo in *The Heart of Anger*

21

Time for Tea

Maggie and her daughter Elise were working diligently throughout the week to prepare for their semi-annual neighborhood tea party. It had become a tradition for this mother and daughter duo to host a gathering of neighborhood moms and their daughters each spring and fall in their home for an afternoon of conversation and delectable edibles. Maggie, who lived on the far end of the furthermost street in their small nook of a neighborhood, always treasured her privacy. She felt the extra bit of distance between her home and her neighbors' a positive attribute because of its location. Maggie never had to concern herself with problems some of her friends seemed to encounter, such as an especially unruly child latching onto their kids. Maggie was grateful for that extra measure of protection she could offer her children simply because of location.

Then one day Maggie had a complete turnaround in her attitude. She and her children had been riding their bikes through the neighborhood when she overheard yelling and fussing coming from inside one of the homes, the one with the blue door. By the time Maggie had passed by the house in question, not only were yells emitting from within, but Maggie heard the loud crash of something breaking, followed by the slam of a door. Out ran a preteen boy. At that moment, Maggie's spirit sunk. What she had always thought a blessing—her set-apart home—wasn't such a positive thing now. Maggie realized how out of touch she was with her neighborhood family. She felt ashamed that she didn't even know the names of those living behind the blue door. How could she pray effectively for this family if she didn't even know who they were? Maggie started to consider ways to get in touch with her neighbors more consistently. After a few feeble overtures, Maggie decided to treat the ladies in her neighboring homes as she'd like to be treated. What better than an afternoon being spoiled and pampered and in the company of other women?

Be hospitable to one another without complaint. As each one has received a special gift, employ it in serving one another, as good stewards of the manifold grace of God.
—1 PETER 4:9–10

Dear Lord, what a lesson I've learned lately. All these years I've been living contentedly, perhaps even a bit smugly. I remember thanking you time and again for protecting me from the hassles my friends experience with troublesome kids they have to deal with day in and day out. But I've been missing the point. You've been urging me to get out of my cocoon and reach out to the families around me. I'm so tunnel-visioned with my homeschooling work that it took an explosive situation played out right in front of me before I even realized what you were trying to communicate to me. I've been a teacher within my home for a long while, perhaps now I'm to be the student for a time, too. I'm so very ashamed of my callousness. Lord, please forgive me. I admit, I have been selfish, comfortable, and oh so complacent.

Please soften this hardened heart of mine. Give me the grace I need to extend myself in genuine caring service to those around me. Lord, I have always taught my children to think of the other person, to let go of personal desires, to give even when it hurts. I have been a hypocrite. I can't even pin-point when I started harboring this "leave me alone" mentality. But it is surely ingrained now. Lord, do your work of sanctification within my heart this day. Renew my mind and stir up my soul. As you have demonstrated so many times, in so many ways, let my life likewise be a sacrificial offering poured out for others. Allow me the privilege of following in your stead. I thank you for your forgiveness and for new beginnings. Awaken my heart with a constant desire to love those whom you've placed within my circle of influence. For your glory, I ask these things. Amen.

Do something—one thing—that defies common sense but makes utter biblical sense. Give something away that we still need but someone else needs more.
—Liz Curtis Higgs in *Mad Mary*

22

No Slipping and Sliding Allowed

Under direct instructions to complete his spelling assignment, ten-year-old Zach mumbled and grumbled for over an hour. This particular ten-year-old despised spelling. He hated trying to neatly copy his vocabulary words on a separate sheet of paper. He dreaded doing the worksheets that helped him use the words in context. But most especially, Zach bucked against writing each spelling word in a complete sentence, one that he had to develop and punctuate correctly on his own. After five years of having his mom as his teacher, Zach knew she'd make him complete the task right down to the last word on his list. Still, Zach was always looking for a way out. While his mom, Jill, was in the next room reading to his sister, Zach decided to try another ploy. He wouldn't complain anymore; he wouldn't say a single word in argument. He would simply do his work at breakneck speed and be done with it.

Jill, who had not heard any recent negative comments coming from the kitchen where Zach was working, wondered whether her son had already completed his lesson. It normally took him a full thirty minutes each day to finish his spelling work, after he quit fuming. Once Jill finished reading a stack of preschool-level books to her daughter, she reentered the kitchen, just as Zach was shutting his book and folder. "Done already?" she queried. He nodded. "That's great, Zach."

She should have known better. Jill turned to set her hand at another task before settling down to check all her son's work for the day. Then a niggling thought entered her mind. How did Zach get done so fast? Jill grabbed the spelling workbook and his folder and began checking the day's lesson. Amazing, Jill thought. He actually did all the work in record time, now if it were neat enough for me to read I might even be able to see if what he did is correct! "Zach, come in here, please," Jill called.

Finally then, brethren, we request and exhort you in the Lord Jesus, that, as you received from us instruction as to how you ought to walk and please God (just as you actually do walk), that you may excel still more.
—1 THESSALONIANS 4:1

Dear Lord, It is a wonder to me that we actually do accomplish our educational goals some days. I often seem to spend more time working on issues of the heart than academics. When I see my children attempting to slide something by that isn't done correctly, I have to intervene. As a parent, I must walk them through the repercussions of handing in shoddy work. Lord, this takes so much of my emotional energy. I am often tempted to just let it slide, even to pretend that I didn't notice the careless effort they put forth. Then I sense you nudging me to address the issue once more. In this I need help. Frequently, I push away your small, still voice and go on to other tasks. This is wrong of me, I admit. Lord, as my children's teacher and their mother, I must see to all sides of these problems. I have to be ready and willing to take steps to ensure they'll do their level best each and every day. Just as your word instructs us to always strive for excellence, so must I. So must my children. Show me how to make them understand that giving their finest effort is not only an exercise of the will but also a moral issue—one that will serve to make or break them. Help them see that we cannot separate our deeds from our very heart and soul. Please give me the words that will impart lasting truth into my kids' lives. My goal for them is not simply to grow academically but also be strong in every aspect of their beings. I truly require that stick-with-it attitude that only you can provide. Lord, I am your child, under your instruction, be my teacher in all things pertaining to my family. Amen.

> If you and I are going to meet the needs of others, we must not view people as interruptions. We must be willing to see them from God's perspective, and we must be willing to help meet their needs.
> —ANNE GRAHAM LOTZ IN *Just Give Me Jesus*

23

Raise Your Right Hand, Please

*T*welve-year-old Kelsey struggled with her accelerated mathematics program. Each day, Kelsey tried working through the text and completing her daily assignment on her own. Each evening, her father arrived home and would answer Kelsey's questions and prepare her for the following day's work. Kelsey's mom, Becky, loved this system. It gave her husband a chance to monitor Kelsey's progress and they both kept a pulse on Kelsey's development. Becky also appreciated her husband's assistance because she was "mathematically challenged," as she jokingly reminded them. Becky's only active participation in the area of math was to grade Kelsey's lessons. After Kelsey finished her lesson, Becky would use the teacher's edition to carefully mark each incorrect answer or place a question mark next to problems she wasn't quite sure about. A few times, Becky was in the midst of grading her daughter's work and the telephone rang. Becky took the call when necessary and occasionally motioned for Kelsey to complete the grading on her own. Becky, who couldn't wait to get the assignment over with for the day, gladly agreed to check her work. Over time, Becky admitted she had virtually given the daily task of checking math work over to Kelsey altogether.

A few months into the school year, Becky's spouse came to her puzzled. It seemed that Kelsey was falling behind. She didn't understand the material as she had earlier in the year. Had Becky noticed any difference in the way Kelsey was tackling her work? Becky couldn't think of any change, so she decided to take a more careful look at Kelsey's workbook the following day. After perusing the pages, Becky started to see a pattern. In the last few weeks, the problems weren't written out in full. It appeared that Kelsey had simply copied the answers. Becky's heart sunk to a new low. How could this be? Would Kelsey have actually taken the answer key and cheated? Becky knew she and her daughter would soon be embroiled in a lengthy heart-to-heart conversation. Then Kelsey's dad would have to be told as well. Much to Kelsey's chagrin, today's mathematics lesson would not soon be over.

Finally, brethren, whatever is true, whatever is honorable, whatever is right, whatever is pure, whatever is lovely, whatever is of good repute, if there is any excellence and if anything worthy of praise, let your mind dwell on these things.
—PHILIPPIANS 4:8

Dear Lord, my system took a jolt this afternoon. I never would have dreamed that my darling child would lie to us. We have always been so close, so honest with our feelings.

This has taken me aback. I almost feel like I'm in shock. How can this be happening in our family? I realize that it's not the end of our world, but real trust has been shattered. I have always had complete confidence in my child. Now I have to step back and reevaluate. What grieves me most is that she would do something wrong in a repetitive manner. This wasn't simply a momentary lapse in judgment but premeditated, day after day. Oh Lord, help me find the right spirit with which to draw my child back to the truth. Give me the words that will speak to the heart. I pray that my youngster is grieving this poor choice. Open the soul's window to your spirit, Lord. Touch the heart and let genuine regret do its redemptive work. I ask that you continue to work in my life as well. Reach down to me in my confusion and help me focus upon your word of hope, your promise of provision. I cannot imagine what went through my child's mind as she attempted to sidestep her work. Lord, I am so saddened. I want to trust again. But I know that it will take time on both our parts before we overcome this obstacle. Please give us what we need to restore our relationship and to protect ourselves from temptation in the coming days. Help me focus on the positive and do not allow this mistake to dampen the spirit of love within our home. Let forgiveness abound. Amen.

> *Lying isn't a matter of degrees. A lie is a lie. And truth is the truth. You can bank on it!*
> —God's Little Devotional Journal for Women

24
I'll Teach You

$\mathcal{S}$omeone knocked on the door just as Tracey was in the middle of mixing the batch of cookie ingredients. She was teaching her daughter about the importance of understanding fractions in cooking. Tracey marked the line on the recipe card so she wouldn't forget just where they stopped and left the room. When Tracey got to the door it was a good neighbor-friend who wanted to drop off a forgotten coat left at her house. All in all, the conversation lasted about fifteen minutes. When Tracey reentered the kitchen, she was surprised to see her son and daughter already placing a tray of cookies into the oven. "You're done?" She queried. "Did you follow the directions carefully? Made sure you included all the correct measurements of ingredients?" Both heads shook in agreement. "Well, then," Tracey marveled, "I guess we'll just wait for the first batch to come out and then we'll taste test your handiwork." As the timer ticktocked through the remaining nine minutes of baking time, Tracey and her two children cleaned up the kitchen. They got everything put away, scrubbed the counters, and even loaded the dishes before the timer went off.

With careful attention, Tracey's kids removed the warm cookies from the oven and transferred them to the cooling rack. They look good, Tracey thought to herself. Recalling other times when vital ingredients had been left out or added in inappropriate amounts, Tracey was impressed with today's evident success. "Get the glasses and the milk," Tracey instructed. A few minutes later, Tracey and her kids were enjoying a short break from their lessons. As Tracey nibbled on a cookie, she praised her children for their good work. Then it hit her; Tracey remembered why they had made the cookies in the first place. She had wanted to take extra time explaining the concept of fractions to her daughter. Well, it's never too late for a lesson, she decided. "Hey, kids, how about I go over the whole fractions lesson right now?"

"No need," they chimed in. "We did that already!"

Looking at her son, Tracey asked, "You actually took the time to explain fractions to your sister?"

"Yeah, and she got it too." He beamed.

"Wow, I'm impressed," Tracey rejoined. "Thank you."

Hear, my son, your father's instruction
And do not forsake your mother's teaching.
—PROVERBS 1:8

Dear Lord, I want to give you thanks for how blessed my heart is today. Most of the time I never really see how my words and efforts are affecting my children. It's difficult to discern whether they're truly allowing my teaching to take root within their hearts. Yet this afternoon, I was so uplifted. Without even a word, my children carried on just as if I had been present with them. They were continuing the work I had begun. This is too wonderful for words. That my child would set aside his own assignments to help his sibling, of all things, astounds me. That he would do so without my prompting makes it all the more precious. Lord, I thank you for giving my child that little heart-nudge to do what was right. And I praise you for your good work I see being accomplished within our homeschool. So many days, I'm unsure about the progress we're making. All it takes is one of these uplifting episodes and I can see how marvelously you are working in my children's lives. You know I esteem a good education, yet all the more I desire for my children's characters to emulate Christ's. These small steps bring me hope that my children are learning to think of others before themselves. I am so very encouraged. I thank you for allowing me to witness this small measure of growth within my children's hearts and lives. Help us continue on this good path. Light our way as we seek to bring glory and honor to your name. It is for your sake we pray, Lord remake us into the image of Jesus. Amen.

> Good habits are what character is all about. The more a person exercises himself for the purpose of godliness, the more godly he becomes. The more godly (like Christ) he becomes, the more he acquires the character of Christ.
> —LOU PRIOLO IN *Teach Them Diligently*

25

Do You Hear Me?

Paige raised her eyebrows in exasperation and mentally counted to ten. It had already been a very tedious morning of grading papers, rechecking mistakes, and tabulating her children's progress. Although Paige loved having her children in the home to school and teach them, she was finding an unexpected challenge in her youngest son. No matter how she approached Jon, he balked at the assignments she handed out. It made little difference how difficult or simple the task; Jon found something to be disagreeable about. If Paige told him to redo a math assignment because it was clear he didn't understand a new concept, Jon cried unfair. When Paige requested that Jon hand in a complete list of spelling words along with an accompanying list of vocabulary sentences, Jon fussed. At first, Paige didn't really notice the subtle changes in her son's attitude. She would correct him and insist that he follow through with her requests. Finally, after days of listening to Jon gripe about the smallest issues, Paige realized her small incremental efforts to reprove Jon weren't working.

The following morning started out as usual. Paige got everyone going on the morning's lessons and then asked Jon to follow her. Once they were privately seated in the family computer room, Paige pulled out her Bible and asked Jon to read a few verses. Then she asked Jon to interpret. What did these words mean to him, specifically? Were his recent attitudes mirroring obedience or disregard to these principles? In what ways should he change both in attitude and action? Jon, who already was quite familiar with these precepts, which spoke of honoring his parents, shrugged. Paige could tell it was going to be a long conversation. But Paige was determined for Jon to come to grips with the fact that he wasn't holding her in a position of respect. As his teacher and his mother, Paige wore both hats with equal authority and each one vested her with the responsibility of training her children. Although Jon may not always want to listen to his teacher-mother, he was compelled by a higher law to obey. If Paige couldn't get through to Jon, she was certain that her husband would.

Children, obey your parents in the Lord, for this is right.
—EPHESIANS 6:1

Dear Lord, it's been another one of those mornings. I'm already depleted of the little reserve of emotional energy I have. Though I can't quite put my finger on the root problem, something is very much amiss with my child. This change has me confounded. My normally complacent youngster is working against my best efforts to instruct him both during school and after. Why he is challenging my authority as his teacher, I'm not sure. Somehow, he's gotten the idea that he has the right to declare his own opinions even at the expense of being disrespectful toward me. This new twist to our relationship has me baffled. I need your wisdom, Lord, to understand how to best communicate my child's offense to him. Undertake with me to bring genuine regret for his heart attitudes and soften the places within him that are hardened against my directives. I know that rebellion often lies just under the surface for many people, but I ask that you bring your truth and light to shine within the knowledge of his heart. Help us work through this difficulty and emerge closer and more united than before. Let not my patience wear to a point of anger. Enable me to communicate to my son in a respectful manner, even when he chooses to address me disrespectfully. I pray that all my words are full of loving instruction and admonition. I also ask for your grace to help me be ready to forgive him quickly. Let not lingering bitterness dwell in either of our hearts. Lord, I commit this parent and teacher relationship to you now, acknowledging that you alone are the true healer of broken spirits and lives. Make your truth be the light we endeavor to follow in all our encounters. Amen.

When we have been broken at Calvary we must be willing to put things right with others—sometimes even with the children. This is, so often, the test of our brokenness. Brokenness is the opposite of hardness. Hardness says, "It's your fault!" Brokenness, however, says, "It's my fault."
—ROY HESSION IN *The Calvary Road*

26

Assistance, Please

$\mathcal{A}$s Danielle listened to her friends proudly regaling the interaction between their husbands and their respective children, Danielle felt a familiar stab of jealousy. She tried to squash this feeling to no avail. It was difficult enough trying to homeschool her five children without any help from her husband. But when Danielle was forced to listen to other moms tell "trophy" tales while she was left to smile at the appropriate intervals, Danielle's heart raged with resentment. She should have known better than to expect her spouse to lend a hand with some of the schoolwork. He had made it perfectly clear from the outset that Danielle was free to teach their kids in the home but he had no interest in taking up a second, part-time tutorial job in the evenings to help her. Danielle, who had feared her husband wouldn't even consider the idea of homeschooling, quickly agreed to his terms. "It's your responsibility, not mine," he warned. Danielle still had forged ahead and made plans to school their children in the fall.

Now four years later, Danielle is still teaching her kids and glad of it. But she's never stopped hoping her husband would have a change of heart. She continues to drop subtle hints about what other dads are doing to help supplement their children's studies. She casually leaves lying around the kitchen homeschooling science retreat flyers that are aimed at fathers and their kids. Danielle occasionally even point blank begs her spouse to offer her some respite. Still, he holds firm. Even Danielle's tears of frustration bring no relief. Danielle certainly could use some assistance. But even she admits that it's not right for her to expect help when she knew from the get-go her husband wasn't willing to get involved. Danielle's cries for help were only causing a further wedge between her and her spouse. He felt she was playing foul by asking for help after they'd already agreed she'd do the work on her own. Although neither one felt reasonably treated, both could use a refresher course in better listening skills.

Love . . . does not take into account a wrong suffered.
—1 Corinthians 13:5b

Dear Lord, I'm not quite certain how I should begin this prayer. I know what I want to happen in my marriage. I desire a real change to take place in the manner in which my husband and I communicate. I feel so misunderstood and wronged. Lord, you know how hard I work each day to accomplish all that needs to be done. I rarely take a break. Whole days go by without my even sitting down. This is so difficult for me. I long for my spouse to express his gratitude for the work I accomplish. But he doesn't. Then I pull away. It's been years, and still we argue over the same homeschooling issues. I admit that I was more than willing to agree to homeschool our children independent of his help. At the time,

I was so overcome by joy to have his OK to proceed; I didn't consider that I would need his input. I feel so cheated, especially when I have to listen to other moms tell about their spouses' involvement. Doesn't my husband care about his children's progress? Why won't he partner with me in this? Lord, I'm at a loss to understand him. I'm also dealing with escalating resentment. Help me refocus on serving my family instead of being served. I know that you will provide everything I require to manage my household. You alone are my right hand of strength. As I strive to push past grievances, help me see the best in my husband. He has so many worthy attributes. Teach me to concentrate on the good he brings to our family. Let not my expectations, reasonable or not, rule my thoughts and emotions. Again, I entrust my desires to you, Lord. Guard my heart against presumptuous sins and enable me to walk in a manner pleasing to you. Amen.

Biblical love paints the other person in the best possible light.
—MARTHA PEACE IN *The Excellent Wife*

27
Step Up the Pace

Gingerly, Emma stepped on her bathroom scale and cautiously peered down at the ominous, bold, black digital numbers callously proclaiming her failure. "Up two pounds!" she screeched. "How can I have gained two more pounds when I've been eating virtually nothing?" Emma shoved the scale against the sideboard and proceeded to get dressed. Ugh. "What is happening to my body?" she lamented. "I can't even contemplate a bowl of ice cream without putting on another pound. Something's definitely amiss here."

Without further debate or self-depreciation, Emma decided upon a totally new course of action. Let's see, she tabulated, I've been married for thirteen years, been having babies for four of those years, nursing for another four years, and I've put on two pounds a year. So, thirteen years means twenty-six extra pounds. At this rate, I'll be weighing-in heavier than I was even at my top pregnancy weight before I even reach age fifty. Something's got to give. I've no more handy excuses left; I'm not carrying a child, not nursing, certainly not sick. I've been meaning to put the kids on a regimented exercise program as well. Maybe we can find something to do together. Walking, biking, or an aerobics video—surely rotating these activities would make everyone happy. I'll see what they'd like to try first. I'm guessing I'll get no protests from any of them. What could be better than a nice, energizing break in the middle of the school day? If we stay on task and exercise for thirty minutes every weekday, I'll venture I won't be dreading my morning weigh-in for very long. After all, how can I expect my children to take good care of themselves when I'm playing the "Do as I say, not as I do" game?

Discipline yourself for the purpose of godliness; for bodily discipline is only of little profit, but godliness is profitable for all things, since it holds promise for the present life and also for the life to come.
—1 TIMOTHY 4:7–8

Dear Lord, I'd like to ask your forgiveness for the miserable example I've set for my kids. I haven't cared for myself in the way I should. I've been quite remiss in exercising and I've not been careful enough in my eating habits. I suppose that convenience often wins out with me in regard to food. I have to admit that I'm often in such a hurry I don't take the time to plan and prepare meals as I should. But I'm most concerned with how this lack of discipline affects me spiritually. I am not content with my portion frequently; I use food as a buffer against emotional stress. Lord, what kind of role model am I setting for my children when they see me turning to quick fixes for comfort instead of you? I realize that I have been pulled in many directions. Still, will there ever be a time when life won't be full of stress? Hardly. I need to place more effort into caring for this body you've given me. I sometimes am afraid that if I don't take the time now while I'm still young, that there will be no more second chances later on. These little concessions I make for my behavior have to stop. It's embarrassing for me to think about how lax I've been while simultaneously teaching my kids their health lessons! Talk about hypocritical. Although they're too polite to say anything, I'm sure they've noticed mom isn't in the peak of fitness. Lord, this is going to be a huge hurdle for me to overcome. Are you with me? It's going to take not only self-restraint but also determination beyond what I can muster up. Lord, it will be your grace alone that will see me through. I know I can count on your faithful hand to guide me. I'm just afraid I'll give up before I've even started. Please show me how to live in ways that enhance life both spiritually and physically. Amen.

When you take control of your physical appetite, you develop strength to take control of your emotional appetite.
—Elmer L. Towns in *Fasting for Spiritual Breakthrough*

28
My Pleasure

*O*n the first Tuesday of every month, Jayne and her three daughters join a group from their church to meet at a nearby nursing home. At precisely 10:00 A.M., Jayne's daughters play piano, violin, and cello as a trio. The girls practice throughout the week, often gathering in the living room after dinner to work on a new piece for their monthly "recital." After playing their part, other members from Jayne's church take turns singing, acting out a comedy routine, or perhaps reciting a poignant story. An informal snack and chat session follows the program. By 11:30 A.M., Jayne rounds up her daughters, whom she finds frequently deep in discussion with the various residents. They pack up their instruments and head home for lunch and then delve into their regular schoolwork.

Each month as Jayne drives home, she marvels at how sensitive her girls have become. They all take it upon themselves to initiate conversations among the men and women who live in the private care facility. It makes Jayne proud to see how much they've matured. She still recalls having had to almost drag the girls into the nursing home the first few times they served there. Her children cried, complained, and tried to cajole Jayne out of making them participate. But Jayne didn't relent. She told them that part of the benefit of being homeschooled is being able to serve in the community on a regular basis. Unlike many other children, their schedules were more easily adapted. Jayne also wanted her girls to learn early on the joy of extending oneself into unfamiliar territory and watching how God works. It was such a satisfying experience for Jayne as she observed the changes in her daughters as they took small steps of faith and reached out in compassion and care to those around them. Jayne also liked to believe that at last, all the music lessons were beginning to pay off.

But now we have been released from the Law, having died to that by which we were bound, so that we serve in newness of the Spirit and not in oldness of the letter.
—ROMANS 7:6

Dear Lord, I am immensely grateful that this opportunity to share and serve arose. For some time I have wanted my children to find a special place where they might serve in our community. It was a heaven-sent arrangement when we joined this group of volunteers. What I am so excited about is that my family is learning how blessed they are! By witnessing the sadness and frailty of others, my children are learning to not take their health for granted. They're also learning what genuine empathy is all about. I cannot count the times when one of my youngster's eyes have overflowed with tears of compassion. This is a bittersweet gift, I know.

I, too, am filled with humility. My heart breaks for the lonely and the crippled. Yet I understand that life never

stands still. Aging is a part of living. Death, too, is eventual.
But for my young children to see past the wrinkles, the
hunched backs, and the loss of memory and bestow love,
kindness, and attention on these folk, it warms my heart.
Perhaps I am most grateful that my family now wants to
serve among the needy. It is no longer necessary for me to
prod and prompt them to do the right thing. You have
sparked a fire within their hearts to desire this responsibility.
Thank you, Lord, for bringing new depth and understanding
to my family's life. Help us continue serving you with the
cheerful heart you so desire us to adopt. Let us be your con-
duit of love, touching, caring, and serving all those we meet.
Amen.

   Christianity is a religion of concern for others.
   —DONALD S. WHITNEY IN *Ten Questions to Diagnose*
   Your Spiritual Health

29

Unfamiliar Territory

Jan called the township hall office and inquired about the summer baseball league sign-ups. She wrote down the dates and also marked them on her calendar. Secretly, Jan hoped some natural disaster might flatten the building before registration. Jan felt miserable whenever she happened to think about summer baseball. Not being a particularly sports-minded person, Jan was out of her element when it came to holding a candle next to other the passionately devoted soccer, swimming, and baseball moms. It made Jan nervous, all this competition. Jan tried to sit on the far ends of the cheering sections and silently endured game after game. Often Jan wondered who wanted to win more, the kids or their parents? Although Jan would have rather done anything but watch her sons participate in these community sports teams, Jan's husband felt otherwise. "They're boys, Jan. It will do them good to mix with other kids they don't know." But, at what cost, Jan questioned.

One of her sons loved every sport on the planet. Whatever it was, he was happy. Jan's older son was the complete opposite. He would rather trek into the woods and spend the afternoon building a tree fort or go fishing than spend his afternoons on a dusty baseball diamond.

Jan tried to see her husband's point of view. It was true that the boys did develop more muscle after spending seven weeks in the company of their peers. But Jan wasn't thinking about their physiques, she only noticed how both her sons grew in emotional and spiritual maturity. Jan's sons amazed her at times. They not only exercised their bodies, they were exercising their faith as well. Overall, Jan had to admit that neither boy ended the season with any lasting scars. But, Jan thought darkly, there's always a first time.

Let your light shine before men in such a way that they may see your good works, and glorify your Father who is in heaven.
—MATTHEW 5:16

Dear Lord, some days I don't think it's possible for me to move farther afield from the competitive sports world than I already am. I have to be truthful: I really don't see the benefit. Perhaps it's just my mother's heart rearing its protective tendencies. But I do know one thing, when kids want to win at any price, it's not worth the sacrifices they're willing to pay. I've seen these young people scream, throw tantrums, swear, and even punch their opponents in a fit of fury.

In all fairness, I realize I also have to try to see the positive sides of these activities. My children have witnessed both good and bad behavior over the years—no different from what they experience in our own neighborhood. And they have demonstrated uncanny ability to handle some pretty sticky situations. I'm very pleased with how they respond to the occasional unkindness and undeserved retaliation. It does my heart good to see them standing firm for what they believe is right. Maybe, as a homeschooling mom, I'm just out of the loop. Other moms face these same issues day in and day out at their children's schools. Me, I can protect my loved ones from most of the peer-inflicted pain. But am I right in doing so? Aren't we to live our faith freely and openly amid our community? This is a difficult step for me to take, Lord. I believe that as long as I am taking care to watch over them, I can give them more independence. As they demonstrate wisdom to make right choices, they should be trusted with more responsibility. I know I'll take two steps forward and then fall back again. Lord, I only ask one thing. Let not fear restrain me from allowing my own light shine into the dark world of so many hopeless families. Enable me to set aside my own discomfort and seek to serve and reassure those around me. Amen.

We don't understand everything, but in the midst of our uncertainty and grief, we choose to embrace life and to lift our eyes and our hearts and our children to the Light of the world. His love is so big that it infiltrates even the darkest valleys.
—SHEILA WALSH IN *A Love So Big*

PART FOUR

Challenges and Choices

The decision to home educate is not always a popular one. Many families face a range of subtle disapproval to outright disdain for their choice. Not everyone will applaud the homeschooling mom's efforts. Still, despite the opposition and hardships, homeschooling families overwhelmingly agree (in hindsight) that they are confident of their decision. Although the homeschooling mom may experience doubts, loneliness, weariness, or isolation, the community of homeschooling families is a growing and supportive one. Seek out those who can offer what you need to succeed. The help is there. You simply need to tap into it.

30
Family Reunion Jitters

Renee reached for her calendar and sighed. Only three more days until her husband's annual family reunion. What should have been cause for celebration turned into a week filled with anxiety. Renee's sister-in-law, Lynn, called her to coordinate the menu items each family was expected to provide for the picnic. Concluding their conversation, Lynn gently broke the news that Renee might want to be prepared for the yearly pep talk on schooling matters. Lynn, bless her heart, tried to soften the blow Renee knew was building within her spouse's extended family. It's happening already, Renee lamented. We're not even at the reunion yet and the family's trying to come up with more ways to persuade us to send our kids to a private school again. Feeling the inner tension mount, Renee decided to step outside and drink in the fragrance from her flower garden. Walking around her back yard, Renee paused. It's amazing that the opinions of one small segment of my world can hold such power over me. We made the decision long ago to homeschool our kids. They've done well— exceedingly so. But no matter what the kids achieve it's never been good enough. Eight years into homeschooling and I still allow myself to get worked up before every family event. This is pointless. It's also a grand waste of my energy and time as well.

"Lord, please hear me now. Help me stay focused on the task at hand—that of managing my home and family. Let me not be ashamed of the choices we've made for our children. As I learn to let go of the opinions of others, you can work through my life more effectively. Teach me not to be afraid but to be firm and stand up for the convictions you've placed upon my heart." Silently, Renee walked back into the house, calmly determined to speak lovingly, yet directly, to each person who chose to challenge her choice of education in the upcoming days.

"And I say to you, everyone who confesses Me before men, the son of Man shall confess him also before the angels of God; but he who denies Me before men shall be denied before the angels of God."
—LUKE 12:8–9

Dear Lord, just a few minutes ago, I learned something about myself. I never would have thought that I was afraid of what others think of me. But I am. I admit it. I've placed the opinions of men above yours, Lord. This is wrong of me. How long have I been so afraid of what people think of us that I lose sight of your calling on my life? My insides just turn to jelly when I recall the emotional exchanges I've had to endure through the years. Yet I shouldn't be so affected. Why do I care if another disagrees with me? When you placed this burden upon my heart to homeschool our children, I was afraid then too. I wasn't sure I was up to the challenge. We started out with little experience, relying heavi-

ly on you for direction. You always provided for my needs as a teacher and for my children as students. I am embarrassed to say that my memory is far too short. I have been on the receiving end of your blessings too numerous to count. Yet I continue to fret and fuss when I am called upon to take a stand. This is a matter of faith for me. I am ashamed of being viewed as extremist or as odd. Forgive me for denying who you've called me to be. I ask you to embolden my heart, but keep my words patient and my temper even-keeled. I want to represent you in a manner that brings glory to your name. On my own, even this is too great an accomplishment for me. I ask that you hold me up and extend your gracious mercy as the needs arise. Amen.

> *The most radical treatment for the fear of man is the fear of the Lord. God must be bigger to you than people are. This antidote takes years to grasp; in fact, it will take all of our lives.*
> —EDWARD T. WELCH IN *When People Are Big and God Is Small*

Dream Stealer

At nineteen years old, Diana got married. At twenty, she gave birth to her first child. By the age of twenty-eight, Diana had five children and another on the way. Despite the cautions Diana and her husband, Rick, received prior to their wedding some nine years before, they had worked hard to develop a strong, viable relationship. Before they married, Diana and Rick agreed that she would work full time until Rick graduated from college. His two-year computer science program would be complete before they had been married a full year. But Diana and Rick hadn't counted on Diana's unexpected "honeymoon" pregnancy. Almost ten months to the day from their wedding, Diana delivered their baby boy. Four others followed in quick succession. Still, Rick had graduated from the junior college as planned and had secured good-paying, steady employment. The rest of Diana and Rick's premarriage (and prechildren) dreams fell by the wayside.

These days, Diana had her hands full juggling the needs of hearth and home. After one particularly grueling morning dealing with the screams of a teething toddler, a feverish four-year-old, and a defiant first grader, Diana threw her hands in the air and gave up. Taking a five-minute bathroom break, Diana closed and locked the door. As she sat down on the floor, hands cradling her throbbing head, Diana let loose and just wept. It had been building, this hopeless feeling of dreams lost. Diana was never one to give in to despair. She coped with any setbacks by digging in and working harder than ever until she felt the wave of disappointment pass. Not this time. Diana was simply worn out. After a few more minutes of solitude, Diana heard little feet make their way to the bathroom, she waited for a frantic knocking, but none came. After a quick rinse of her face, Diana opened the door and spied all five of her children looking at her in expectation. Suddenly amused, Diana laughed and told the kids to get their coats and shoes. "We're going to Grandma's house for the day."

And He said to me, "My grace is sufficient for you, for power is perfected in weakness." Most gladly, therefore, I will rather boast about my weaknesses, that the power of Christ may dwell in me. Therefore I am well content with weaknesses, with insults, with distresses, with persecutions, with difficulties, for Christ's sake; for when I am weak, then I am strong.
—2 CORINTHIANS 12:9–10

Dear Lord, at this moment, I am found wanting. My soul is aching for more than I have; my heart and mind feel cheated over all that I have given up. I look around at my family and all I see is the work I still have to accomplish. I know that you fully understand what drives me. You have given me special gifts and abilities to use in service for you. Yet at this point, I feel stifled. I am not regretting my past choices; still I feel hemmed in by them. The truth is I am constrained by the needs of my family. I also understand that this is not a bad thing. Yet I sometimes wish for an entire day alone—no washing, no cooking, no diapers, no crying, and no responsibilities! Rejuvenate me and let your peace reign supreme in my troubled heart. Give me all I require to mother my children and to instruct them with kindness. Let not my own thwarted desires get in the way of loving those precious ones around me. Lord, you are the only one who can offer up the daily strength I need to continue at this task. Steady me now, and enable me to put my trust in your provision once again. Help me to cling to your promise that in time all things can be made beautiful. Even now, I offer to you the sacrifice of my own dreams. I give them into your keeping until the time is right. I entrust to you the remainder of this day. Please make it count for eternity. Amen.

> *If your happiness comes from something you deposit, drive, drink, or digest, then face it—you are in prison, the prison of want. . . . If you have the Shepherd, you have grace for every sin, direction for every turn, a candle for every corner, and an anchor for every storm.*
> —MAX LUCADO IN *Traveling Light for Mothers*

32
Memo That

*A*mid steaming mugs of hot coffee, assorted plates of breakfast food, and much laughter, Mary and her friends regroup and reevaluate on the first Saturday of every month. At first, the idea of getting up early the one day of the week when all the moms could have had at least a shot at sleeping in seemed foolish. Then, one by one, Mary's monthly breakfast club grew. Some of the moms heard about the previous meeting through mutual friends. A few spoke directly to Mary and were invited to join. Still others found their way through a homeschooling acquaintance. Mary didn't care who showed up at 6:30 A.M. on these first Saturdays. She knew she would make an appearance even if no one else did.

After homeschooling for some five years, Mary was burnt out. No longer did she enjoy the thrill of achievement when one of her children reached a milestone in learning. Mary, like many others, had gotten so used to the status quo, so comfortable in her successful curriculum, even she was bored. Mary's commitment toward homeschooling her kids never wavered. But Mary realized she needed some new ideas, something fresh to offer her children and to help her get excited about the learning process as well. What better resource than her own homeschooling friends? When Mary considered scheduling issues, she decided that one Saturday morning a month would work best. Any meetings had to be in the early morning before the weekend rush began. So Mary put out the word to her friends, got in touch with the restaurant where she wanted to hold the breakfast, and the rest is history. Over two years have passed since that first breakfast club session and Mary continues to see new faces gather around the tables. What amazes Mary the most is that every week she hears a new idea or a fresh take on an old idea. The best part is that Mary and the other moms start out the day with a great breakfast topped off by the finest nourishment of all—the camaraderie born of shared trust and mutual commitment.

Let us consider how to stimulate one another to love and good deeds, not forsaking our own assembling together, as is the habit of some, but encouraging one another; and all the more, as you see the day drawing near.
—HEBREWS 10:24–25

Dear Lord, lately, I've been wondering just how long I'll be able to continue schooling my children at home. In fact, I've been dreaming about the days when I won't be so constrained by their schedules. It's not that I don't love having my children with me during the day. The sad truth is that I've become bored with the process. We've gotten into a pattern that works, true enough. But I'm not challenged any longer. It's been too predictable for too long. Lord, I realize I should be thanking you that we haven't encountered any major problems and I am grateful. Yet I don't feel that I'm exercising my gifts at all. I guess the real truth is that I'm feeling stuck. Help me, Lord, see the good in what I do each day. Reveal to me the eternal effects of teaching my children. My vision is so very shortsighted. I long for a rock solid faith that comes as natural as breathing. Lord, give me the insight I need to work out this temporary setback and enable me to breathe new life into my own homeschool. As I commit my children's education into your faithful keeping, I also ask that you provide me with the life-giving words, which will breathe hope to my friends. I know that I am not alone in my struggles. My friends frequently experience the same frustrations as I do. Be with us, Lord. Please take over and lead us as we endeavor to provide the best education available. Into your care, I give my desires and dreams, my children and their futures, my friends and their families. Amen.

> *Failure is the end of almost every good beginning. God himself had to contend with it almost immediately after creation. But that did not stop him from continuing on, determined to finish what he started.*
> —MARK EDDY SMITH IN *Tolkien's Ordinary Virtues*

33

Blindsided by the Facts

After months of heartache, Kathy, single mom to Jared, decided to pull her son out of the public school where he attended. Kathy spent many hours each day mulling over the changes she'd seen in Jared. Although Kathy's husband had left them some five years earlier, it was just this current school year that Jared started displaying significant problems in his classes and with the other kids. Now twelve, Jared was in junior high school. Kathy worried that she needed to get a handle on Jared's misbehavior now—later would be too late. Even the school counselor recommended a home study program that their system had in place for kids who weren't succeeding in traditional educational settings. Kathy considered this counselor's suggestion, and after talking with friends and family decided to withdraw Jared from his regular classes. Since the holidays were drawing to a close, Kathy felt grateful that Jared could reenroll in this special home study program immediately after winter break. A fresh start, Kathy reminded herself. Both of us have needed that for quite some time.

Kathy was surprised how easily Jared slipped into the routine she set up for him. Jared had no trouble working independently and seemed to relish getting his assignments completed prior to the deadlines. If anyone was struggling now, it was Kathy. She couldn't count the number of times people whom she knew and loved raised their eyebrows in question when Kathy told them what Jared was doing. Everyone seemed to have an opinion and very few of them positive. As a single mother, Kathy already wrestled with decision making and frequently doubted herself. It amazed her that given Jared's prior problems, anyone would find fault with the avenue she had chosen to set matters straight. Why, Kathy wondered, does everyone have to be a critic? Just because they don't understand how homeschooling works doesn't mean it doesn't!

A father of the fatherless and a judge for the widows
Is God in His holy habitation.
—PSALM 68:5

Dear Lord, why am I so misunderstood? I have tried to make the best decisions for my child and me. You know how I labor over every choice presented. I even ask for counsel from those I trust. Still, I feel so condemned. Certainly, my youngster has had problems. It seems that every person I know is aware of this fact. Yet I'm so weary of trying to explain my own choices. I believe this path we're on now is effective. I've seen the evidence of it. This pleases me more than I can say. Thank you for providing this avenue for our family. I am confident that you will continue to work and accomplish good things in my family's life. I ask that you stay close, reach out to the neediness in our souls, and bring a cleansing healing.

You alone are able to make us strong and resilient enough to cope with our pain. One thing I pray is that you never leave us. Be our guide and our reservoir of strength always. I commit my child to you again this day. And Lord, help me handle the unintentional unkindness of others. I understand that they are trying to offer help. Yet their words and their spirit of judgment rest heavily upon me. Protect me from their harshness and do not allow my child to feel their lack of mercy. We have been broken and battered enough already. Our need for you has never been more urgent. Please, Lord, truly take your place as father to my son and be my righteous judge in this difficult place. Amen.

The point is simply this: the greater the odds, the better for God.
—CHARLES STANLEY IN *How to Handle Adversity*

34

Mom of the Moment

Rachel tugged at the stroller, whose wheels had gotten wrenched once again in the uneven sidewalk, while she beckoned to her eight-year-old-son, Kyle, to wait for her. In a rush as usual, Kyle was ignoring her instructions. Just like earlier, Rachel lamented. A few minutes later, Rachel and her three children arrived at their neighborhood park. Each child was eager to try out the newly assembled jungle gym. With Kyle hanging by his hands and six-year-old Abby barreling down a slide at breakneck speed, Rachel had only baby Jess to look after. Rachel relished the moment. She sat next to her ragged stroller, now so worn from use it was more hassle than help when she went out. Jess was happily hitting at the chew toys dangling over her head. With the sun shining and a faint breeze blowing, Rachel could almost, but not quite, push away the memories of their disastrous morning.

Looking around at the nicely kept homes situated around the park, Rachel was reminded of another difficult retreat she took to escape from the kids' outbursts and upsets. It was only about a week ago that Rachel had had her fill of squabbling and complaints. She felt impatient herself, and her children's misbehavior only served to escalate her own frustrations that morning. So in one fell swoop, she had ordered the kids to get their coats and off they went to the park. Not a cure-all certainly, but most definitely a temporary reprieve. As soon as they had arrived, a group of senior ladies strolled by on their morning walk. Of course, they couldn't resist a peek at Jess, who was napping, and they delighted over how well Rachel's older two were getting along as they took turns pushing each other on the swings. "You just have the most perfect family," they cooed. Rachel felt ill. Is that what it looks like? The perfect family? Ha! If only they'd seen me an hour ago when I was right in the thick of what felt like World War III. Amazing, that anyone could actually believe we're the model family.

But God has chosen the foolish things of the world to shame the wise, and God has chosen the weak things of the world to shame the things which are strong.
—1 CORINTHIANS 1:27

Dear Lord, when I read your word proclaiming that you have chosen those who are weak or foolish, I am awed. Your ways are indeed so high above my own, I am overcome by your goodness and mercy. Just today, I have seen more evidence of your compassion toward me. You know how difficult these past days have. My patience level is almost exhausted. My children must sense my irritability as well. Certainly, they are responding to my cues as surely as I am responding in kind to their moods. Help me, Lord. I feel so weak right now. My children are the light of my world. Yet with all the commotion and the noise, I sometimes long for quiet. I can feel myself tensing each time another outburst occurs. It doesn't matter whether or not my children are rambunctiously having fun or in the middle of a spat, the noise level alone sends me spinning. What is the matter with me? I am amazed that others seem to think I've got it all together. If they only knew how I struggle to maintain a calm demeanor! But you know the truth. Be my strength, my guide through this stormy season. I know it will get better. I have to believe that. With your good grace, I can accomplish all that I need to as a mom. I believe it is possible to be with my children around the clock without losing it. Lord, show me ways to make my home a calm, peaceful retreat for my family. And most of all, help me want to be in the midst of that tranquil setting. Amen.

As in all races, the way you finish is always more important than the way you start.
—CYNTHIA SPELL HUMBERT IN *Deceived by Shame, Desired by God*

35

Sick at Heart

Annette studied the reading on the thermometer for the third time in as many hours. Her son, Evan, had been fighting a viral infection for several days, and last evening his temperature shot up to 103.5. Annette gave Evan some children's ibuprofen, pushed the fluids, and slept nary a wink all night. Exhausted from her vigil, Annette's emotional reserves were teetering on empty. Although this particular illness hadn't precipitated a full-blown asthma attack, Annette knew the signs. Evan's allergy and asthma always seemed to come into play whenever he became ill. So Annette watched him carefully. Normally a simple virus didn't affect Annette so drastically, but this school year had been peppered with more "sick days" than regular school days. Annette was getting a tad anxious that all her advanced planning and scheduling to keep Evan on track would soon become moot. Often Annette would wring her hands in worry, fretting in advance about the upcoming testing that their family took part in each spring. Would Evan be ready? Would he score high enough to set Annette's husband at ease? These questions and more loomed large in Annette's mind as she tucked in the blankets around her son's feet and went to retrieve another tumbler of water for him.

It's no good worrying, Annette chided herself impatiently. I've got to look at this situation realistically. If Evan had been in public school all year, he would have fallen miserably behind. No doubts about that. Teaching him at home has been a good thing. At least Evan's been able to stay current with all his reading assignments. And I've been keeping him up to speed by reading his history and health lessons as well. No more fretting, Annette, you're simply wasting precious energy on a futile attempt to make the untamable issues of life more manageable.

If you are slack in the day of distress,
Your strength is limited.
—PROVERBS 24:10

Dear Lord, I would love nothing better than to come before your throne with a heart full to the brim with thanksgiving and praise. I long for my heart to overflow with joyous adoration again. Yet in truth my mind is struggling to keep calm. I'm feeling so overwhelmed by the countless times my child has been ill this year, so many I cannot number them. I have never had such a season of sickness take over our home before. I feel helpless to protect my family against these unseen enemies. It has been a long winter, Lord. Now I am ready for a new season of wellness to take residence here. Please help me overcome my anxieties; they are threatening to pull me under. It is enough that I am called upon to care for my family— this alone exhausts me. But now I'm under an attack of my own making! My very thoughts combat what I know to be true. Lord, help me focus upon the promised provision found in your word. Protect my thoughts against negativity and feelings of hopelessness. Give me what I require to offer ongoing encouragement to my child, too. In my moments of self-absorption, I have neglected his struggle to get well. I have been selfishly consumed with my own comfort and desires. Please help me put my energies into offering generous doses of comfort and care to my needy child. Together, help us look to you for our strength. I realize I need to place my eyes upon Christ this day. May my focus, my concentration rest upon you rather than my pitiful circumstances. Will you do this good work within me, even now? Lord, move more deeply into my heart and root out what is displeasing to you. Make me into a woman of faith, a mother with vision, and as a child who trusts in you unreservedly. Amen.

If your life is only producing a whine, instead of the wine, then ruthlessly kick it out.
—OSWALD CHAMBERS IN *My Utmost for His Highest*

36

The Bitter and the Sweet

*I*t was almost 4:00 P.M., school was over for the day, dinner was simmering on the stove, and the children were outside enjoying the unseasonably warm weather. With a few minutes of solitude, Kelly decided to tackle the field trip release forms she had been putting off. With three children heading off to camp once summer came, Kelly needed to get their registration forms filled out and into the mail the following morning. They won't forgive me if I don't get these to the registrar before the slots fill up, Kelly told herself pointedly. Kelly was surprised how quickly she breezed through the questionnaires, recalling that some forms were absolute nightmares to complete. As she got to the bottom, where emergency contact information was required, Kelly by habit began to write her mother's name, address, and telephone number. Then she paused. Tears welled up in Kelly's eyes, which she hurriedly wiped away.

Her concentration broken, Kelly thought back over the past six months. With no prior warning, Kelly's once healthy mom became ill. After numerous tests and weeks of uncertainty, the doctor's grim diagnosis had torn their family apart. Cancer. How that single word would alter their lives forever. Kelly couldn't believe it had been only six months. It was true though, twenty-four nightmarish weeks of agony that swept through Kelly's entire family. Now it was over. Kelly felt grateful that her mom wasn't suffering any longer. Yet Kelly found it difficult to forge ahead with her life. She was constantly fighting tears, battling depression, and on edge with her kids. Kelly tried to press forward one day at a time, but the pain was almost suffocating. It seemed that the least event would trigger a crying jag or worse. Kelly couldn't count the number of afternoons she pleaded a killer headache and retreated into her bedroom to be alone. No matter where she was, no matter what she did, Kelly couldn't escape the fact that her mourning was threatening to engulf her. Unable to think straight, Kelly pushed aside the camp forms for another time, another day. She shook herself as she remembered her momentary lapse with regret. "And it had been such a good day," she said.

───────────────────────────────

But He gives a greater grace.
—JAMES 4:6

Dear Lord, today I thought I had it made. I really believed I would make it through the day without falling apart. But it didn't happen. Once again, just a reminder of how life has changed, and I fell to pieces. I know that grieving is a good thing. Lord, help me cope with this loss. My own children are suffering because I'm so entrenched in my own sorrow. Some days I can't summon up the energy to even do our school assignments. I just can't think straight. I know this frightens them, too. My edginess is about to drive everyone out of the house as well.

What can I do to turn a corner and let my grief take its course without incapacitating me? I'm so afraid of my own despair. Life just doesn't seem worth living anymore. Lord, I'm clinging to you with the finest shreds of faith. But it's all I can muster up. I'm asking you to give me whatever it is that I require to get past this dark place. Help me, please. Your promises assure me that you are able to give me the grace to overcome my adversities. Never before have I needed that generous gift as right now. I ask you to be true to your word, as I know you always are, and come to my aid. Indeed, rescue me from this pit of despair. Let me soon see new days in which I can praise your name. Amen.

Sometimes the darkness around us is not a darkness of death but rather a darkness like in a womb, where we are growing and being made ready for birth.

—STORMIE OMARTIAN IN *Lord, I Want to Be Whole*

37

Divisive Decisions

Debbie sat on her front porch and swung back and forth on the porch swing. To anyone who might be watching, Debbie appeared to be enjoying a few moments of respite after a long day working outside in the yard. That assessment was in part accurate. Debbie had spent the day weeding, mowing, and trimming bushes right alongside her husband Jake. It had been a long day, too. But what no one else knew was that Debbie wasn't simply resting, she was agonizing over Jake's decision to put their son into public school in the fall. Debbie never expected this bombshell. While Debbie rocked back and forth her mind followed suit. Her thoughts raced from one possible reason to another. Still, she couldn't figure out what had precipitated this about-face from Jake. Hadn't they discussed that they would be homeschooling throughout high school? Weren't they currently investigating some new upper-level materials for next year? Wasn't their name on the list at the upcoming conference for homeschooling at the high school level? It didn't make any sense. Nor had Jake's quick dismissal of the subject. Debbie was at a loss to understand this turn of events. And what will Brian say? Debbie could barely contain her emotions. Each fresh thought brought more frustration and irritation. How could he do this to us? What was he thinking? And when am I going to get the answers I need to help me work this through?

Alarmed that Jake wasn't interested in conversing more freely, Debbie decided to try a different tack. She'd calm down before bringing up the subject again. She'd pray it through on her own before broaching any further conversation. Maybe if she just cooled down and let Jake see she could discuss the problem calmly, he'd be more willing to open up. Alternately frantic and frazzled, Debbie decided to stay put for the time being. Another half an hour or so of focused relaxation might not be such a bad idea given Debbie's present volatile mind-set.

Our flesh had no rest, but we were afflicted on every side: conflicts without, fears within. But God, who comforts the depressed, comforted us.
—2 CORINTHIANS 7:5–6A

Dear Lord, be my strength at this moment of utter confusion and strife. Help me calm down, to rest in the security of your provision. I am an emotional wreck right now. Please, Lord, intervene for me in this situation. I fear that the words I utter may only make the situation worse. My emotions are raw and in my heart I am blaming others for my present state. I know I must master my anger and be ready to listen but my heart is crying out for the opposite. Rather, I want nothing more than to declare my own opinions. Lord, help me gain some inner peace and see this impasse in its right perspective. Perhaps I have overreacted, but I am afraid. I felt suddenly shaken by this major twist in our lives. Lord, I need nothing more at this moment than your grace to enable me to speak with respect, tact, and care. Give me what I require to rebuild the relationship I trampled upon earlier with my rashness. Show me how to speak in a manner that communicates my heart accurately and effectively. I pray that we can work through this dilemma and emerge more united than before. I commit this situation, our conversation, and our relationship to your capable hands. Amen.

It is always self who gets irritable and envious and resentful and critical and worried. It is self who is hard and unyielding in its attitudes to others. . . . As long as self is in control, God can do little with us.
—ROY HESSION IN *The Calvary Road*

38

Pennies from Heaven

ooking through the on-sale section at the meat department, Catherine felt stymied. She couldn't decide what cuts of meat to get for the upcoming week. With a very limited food budget and six hungry people, Catherine needed to choose wisely. She picked up a couple of whole chickens for roasting, a three-pound round steak, and five pounds of ground beef. Catherine looked over her grocery list a final time and decided that today's purchases would cover the remainder of the week. Making her way down the nearest aisle to the shortest checkout line, Catherine wondered how much this week's groceries were going to cost. She tried not to fret about money matters, but this had been an especially trying week. All on the same day, Catherine's appliances decided to go kaput. Her refrigerator was freezing the produce, the broiler in her oven shorted out, and her washing machine started hopping all over the basement floor during the rinse and spin cycle. To top off that "breakdown" day, Catherine also called in the furnace repairman to fix a fan that wouldn't stop running and had elevated their electric bill to almost double.

As Catherine neared the cashier, she had to stifle the desire to run home and start perusing the want ads. In moments of financial stress, Catherine felt drawn to the newspaper and would begin searching for a part time nursing position. She knew how much income she could pull in as an RN if she worked even a couple of weekends a month. She also understood that once she went back to work, she'd slowly be pressured into more and more hours away from home. And hadn't she already decided that homeschooling had to take priority over any monetary extras? Did they ever lack for anything they really needed? Was shopping for bargains that much of a sacrifice? Catherine realized any trade-offs were most certainly worth the time she was able to invest in her children's young lives. Before long, they will be grown and gone and then I'll have time and money enough to spare, Catherine told herself.

Let your character be free from the love of money, being content with what you have; for He Himself has said, "I will never desert you, nor will I ever forsake you."
—HEBREWS 13:5

Dear Lord, I had another one of "those" days. I was fretful and anxious and everyone around me knew it. I was doing pretty well handling all the unexpected breakdowns at home. Then it hit me suddenly. In all honesty, I felt panic-stricken. Lord, this is not good. I really believed that I had made definite strides in my heart attitude regarding our limited income. But I continue to balk against any type of financial constraints. Since when did I think that leaving behind a lucrative career to school my children would be without cost?

Our choice to homeschool has been quite costly to our budget. And yet I wouldn't alter our decision. In my heart, I know that the investment I am making in the lives of our family is far beyond any material benefits my working outside of the home can offer. I want to be the one who teaches them about life and learning. But I am also struggling with discontentment and fear. Though you have always provided beyond our needs and graciously given us many of our wants, I still find it so difficult to trust in your provision. Refresh my memory, Lord. Bring to my mind the countless creative measures you have taken to demonstrate your constancy and care. Help me focus upon you alone during my moments of anxiousness. Thank you, Lord, for giving me the desires of my heart and for pressing me to push past the smallness of mind to which I frequently cling. I am blessed both within and without. Let my attitude reflect this knowledge from this day forward. Amen.

At times it is lonely. It's scary. It's unknown. But . . . But . . . Here in all his wonderful grace and glory stands God. He stands up in the broken places. He stands up in broken people. He stands firm on bloodied feet. He stands among us.
—SHEILA WALSH IN *Living Fearlessly*

39

Idling Fast

When Nina heard her son call from his makeshift classroom in their family office, she didn't even attempt to stifle a groan. "Not again," Nina complained. Another question? So soon? I've already been making permanent treks through the carpeting just in the last half hour. A few minutes later, Nina was back in the kitchen looking through her dinner menu when her daughter called for her help. Ugh. Another interruption. Nina traipsed through the living room to her daughter's bedroom, where she was busy writing a report on honeybees. Another few minutes passed and Nina was again flipping idly through her stack of recipe cards. Where is it? Nina frowned in concentration. "Mom!" Aagh. "When will I ever have the opportunity to finish something I've started without being interrupted?" Nina said to no one in particular.

Some ten minutes passed and Nina retreated for a third time into her kitchen, determined to get a head start on dinner preparations. As she tentatively started cutting and chopping for a beef stew she was making, Nina kept her ears tuned for another urgent call beckoning her immediate assistance. When none came, Nina started to unwind. I don't know what's wrong with me lately, she thought. I am so weary of homeschooling, some days I don't think I'll make it through the day. And to think we still have four more months left until the school year is over. I've never felt so disagreeable before. Every time one of the kids calls for help, I'm cringing inside. I can't stand the thought of trying to work through another algebra problem, dissect another frog, or help my daughter rewrite her book report. It's too much. I'm running on empty, I'm burned out, and I don't really care who knows it. Lord, I'm in a sorry state right now and I don't see any relief in sight.

The Lord has given Me the tongue of disciples, that I may know how to sustain the weary one with a word. He awakens Me morning by morning, He awakens My ear to listen as a disciple. The Lord God has opened My ear; And I was not disobedient, Nor did I turn back.
—ISAIAH 50:4–5

Dear Lord, if there was ever a time when I needed to set my eyes upon Christ and emulate his footsteps, it is now. I am floundering through my days and can't seem to keep my head above it all. Everything, my family, my home, the schooling, it is all too much for me to handle. I'm weary beyond measure. In every way conceivable, I'm exhausted. I feel as though I have nothing left to give. I am empty. Poured out, undone, and defeated. Lord, I cannot recall a period in my life when I've ever experienced such overwhelming pressure. I know it's been building for some time, but finally, it has hit me. I can't go on in the same vein as before. I know I don't fully understand what's happening within me, except that I am truly scared that I'll not be able to pull myself out of this pit. Nothing in my life right now gives me satisfaction or pleasure. I can feel myself pulling in tighter by the hour. I want to keep at bay anything or anyone who might place even more expectations upon me. Lord, what's happening to me? Even the children's noise agitates me. I cannot tolerate the constant commotion or the unending demands. I need you, Lord. I've never needed your presence as I do now. Please show me a way out of this dark place. I don't know how much more I can stand. The only truth that gives me comfort is that I know I am your child. I am certain that you will stand with me and guide me out of my pain. Just do not leave me to face these demons alone. Lord, I can only pray that you will come to me at my point of need. If ever I wanted rescuing, it is now. Give me what I require to make it through this day. Amen.

Great heat for plants is like great tension for humans. The next time you're feeling overwhelmed with emotion, remember the lesson of the wallflower. Dehisce. Explode in a way that is productive. Let yourself cry or rock with laughter. It helps.
—JEAN LUSH IN *Women and Stress*

40

It Cuts Both Ways

$\mathcal{D}$uring their monthly homeschooling-planning meeting, one of the moms happened to bring up the newest political issue regarding homeschooling laws in their state. She read the highlights of an article taken from the newspaper and went on to disparage the leaders who felt it necessary to introduce such a law in the first place. Vickie agreed with this mom's assessment. Then the talk turned to the sad state of the public schools across the country. Comments flew from one to another, each mother interjecting her own caustic remarks about teachers, administrators, testing, and the state's interference. No good comes out of the schools, that's for sure, Vickie heard one woman complain.

"Ah, I have to disagree," Vickie spoke up finally. "Remember, my husband is a teacher?" Everyone quieted. Vickie rarely felt compelled to defend the public schools but when homeschoolers box and tag all other forms of education into one package and label them "deficient" because of a few, it isn't right. Vickie scarcely could remember a time when one of the homeschooling moms wasn't complaining about the erroneous assumptions placed on homeschooling families. "We aren't always portrayed accurately, and neither are the public schools," Vickie said. "No one sees how hard my husband works to teach his high school students. No one knows how many hours he spends on evenings and weekends in preparation for his classes. Nor do many homeschoolers realize how much many of the high school kids are learning today." Vickie stopped for a moment, "I think it's a shame when we homeschoolers take the high road and unfairly judge others who have decided to educate their children another way. Aren't we then just as guilty of the same discrimination we complain about?"

Do not judge according to appearance, but judge with righteous judgment.
—JOHN 7:24

Dear Lord, it is remarkable to me that as a homeschooling mom myself, I continue to feel it necessary to defend public and private education. Why is there such dissension between these educators? I understand that our mode of teaching is quite different. But don't we all have the best interests of the children in mind? This growing rift disturbs me. What grieves me most is that many of the homeschooling moms I count as friends are so embittered against any form of schooling not conducted from the home. They cannot or will not admit that some kids thrive in a regular school setting. This is nothing more that discrimination. How can we as homeschoolers cry foul when we're publicly maligned and misunderstood, then do an about-face and render the same judgment on those within the public or private school sector? Perhaps it's because I know many dedicated school teachers that I see both sides. There is no perfect solution in regard to education. Each form has its positive and negatives.

And Lord, I'm ashamed to say that we homeschooling moms are so bold as to even coerce other mothers into following our homeschooling agenda. This decision is too important to be pressured into; each family must prayerfully decide for themselves. It is not pleasing to you, Lord, when we state our beliefs in such a dogmatic manner that we brook no disagreement or reasonable interchange. I think we've become so entrenched that at times we fail to applaud the good things that are happening outside our own four walls. Lord, give us generous and fair spirits. Help us accept others who are different and not judge them for the choices they make. Bring us to a place of common ground and respect, Lord. I pray that homeschoolers not be known by our attitude of exclusivity but by our love. Shine your light of goodwill and concern through our words and our actions. Let no one misunderstand our willingness to serve children, all children, no matter where they are educated. Amen.

A good thing to remember, a better thing to do—work with the construction gang, not the wrecking crew.
—God's Little Devotional Journal for Women

PART FIVE

The Perks

*F*amilies sacrifice in numerous ways to home educate their children. Money is often tight, time is at a premium, energy levels wane, opposition is faced, and doubts loom large. The list can go on and on. Yet with all the struggles comes an abundance of joy, satisfaction, and accomplishment. Few other such decisions can affect the family in such a powerful way as homeschooling. Moms can be there for their children for both quality and quantity time. Children grow up knowing that they are highly valued by their parents. The family unit develops into a team working together, playing together, and serving together.

41

Mission Accomplished

*V*alerie slowly meandered through the exhibit building, amazed at the intricacies and inventiveness displayed before her. Val, who once chaffed at the endless hours her two boys spent on their science fair project because it took so much time away from their other studies, now realized how mistaken she had been. Val's boys weren't trying to get out of their lessons, they knew better than their mom just what was expected of them and how tough the competition would be. Val was so proud. It was one thing for her sons to take the initiative and tackle a difficult task such as an innovative science project that incorporated a variety of academic disciplines; it was quite another for them to dedicate themselves for weeks on end to see this goal to its completion.

As Val worked her way through the expansive building, she felt especially grateful for the homeschooling group she'd joined back in the fall. Shy, reserved, perhaps even a bit standoffish, Val had been on the lookout for homeschooling support for over two years. Her small town didn't contain many homeschoolers, so Val spent more time working out the "wrinkles" of day-to-day schooling on her own. Yearning for some support, Val continued looking for some sort of group that would offer her a listening ear.

After hearing the boys ask for the umpteenth time for some extracurricular club activities, Val turned to the local 4-H organization. Here, Val discovered, was where all the homeschoolers met. Val was elated to join such a solid company of like-minded families, and her sons were ecstatic about the diversity of opportunities available to them. All in all, Val's expectations had been exceeded both academically and socially. It had taken some time, but Val was now reaping benefits untold.

O Thou who dost hear prayer,
To Thee all men come.
—PSALM 65:2

Dear Lord, what a joyous occasion this is for my family and me. I have waited and searched for support for many months now. You have brought us to a place that meets and actually exceeds my desires. I want to thank you for providing this group of moms and their children. They have been more blessing to me than I can tell. It is such a wonderful thing to be able to share with others who are in the midst of similar struggles or joyous celebrations, depending upon the day. I am so taken aback at how much my children have learned this year as well. I have watched other adults step in and guide my youngsters through steps of learning that I am unqualified to teach. Bless them, Lord. For certainly, you have blessed our family through their efforts.

I must also express how grateful I am for your attentiveness to my prayers. Waiting and searching for just the right fit did me a world of good. Even though I was frequently unsure about specific issues, I learned to lean upon you for the answers. It was during my "alone time" that I was schooled in the fine art of faith, trust, and hope. You never failed me and for that I am beyond grateful. I am still awed by your timing and your generous gift of new friends. Your promises of completed provision are trustworthy and true. My faith has been strengthened as I continue to witness the character that is developing in my children. They are stretching and straining to apply excellence in their work. Only to you, Lord, is praise to be given for this lovely change. I ask only one thing now, please continue to strengthen my faith, enlarge my vision, and allow me to bring encouragement to others in the same way my newfound friends have ministered to me. Amen.

> *Children are not raised in thirty minutes. Homeschooling will not change your life in thirty days or your money back. . . . The real treasure is at the end of the road when you have a child who is spiritually mature, academically solid, poised, and able to win the favor of God and man.*
> —MIKE FARRIS IN *The How and Why of Home Schooling*

A New Direction

As Bonnie prepared her children for the homeschooling spring banquet, her stomach twisted into a knot. This was the first time she'd ever had the occasion to attend this "gala" event. Bonnie wasn't too sure she'd fit in with this group of stay-at-home homeschooling mothers and their families. Gathering her daughter's hair ribbons, Bonnie started working on braiding Karly's curly, almost defiant tendrils into a smoothly plaited style. A lot like me, mused Bonnie, as she worked the stubborn strands into place. Getting to her feet, Bonnie gave Karly a final check and ushered her into the living room with strict instructions to sit quietly while she finished everyone else's hair. One by one, Bonnie worked with each child, then fussed at Joe's shirt and straightened his tie. At last, Bonnie hastily closeted herself in her bathroom and gave herself the once over.

Ooh, I am uptight, Bonnie thought as she pressed a palm against her churning abdomen. What exactly am I so afraid of, Bonnie chided. Grimly, she silently reiterated her habitual litany of self-condemnation. Twice married, countless live-in boy friends, recovering prescription drug addict . . . should I continue? Bonnie grilled herself. Looking straight in the mirror, she saw nothing there to compare with the other moms, who knew from the beginning they would homeschool, never worked a day outside their own homes, were still married to their first husbands, and doubtless frowned at taking an aspirin! Feeling overcome by nausea, Bonnie's upper lip crested with a fine line of perspiration. *Great, not only do I not fit the "home-schooling mold," I look the part of a disheveled wreck as well.* Paralyzed by fears of her own making, Bonnie vowed to stay entrenched in the safety of her bathroom for the remainder of the day. But her vow was short-lived when a knock on the door startled her and she heard the words, "Come on, Honey, we need to leave. The Sailors all have the flu and you're filling in on the podium this afternoon. The kids and I are helping hand out the awards." Bonnie couldn't believe her ears. *Of the over one hundred families attending the banquet and she was chosen to take over as hostess? Amazing. OK, Lord, maybe you are trying to tell me that no one else cares about my past anymore than you do.*

If we confess our sins, He is faithful and righteous to forgive us our sins and to cleanse us from all unrighteousness.
—1 JOHN 1:9

Dear Lord, this is so difficult for me to admit. I am still troubled and embarrassed by my past. It didn't seem to matter much to me until I joined this group of mothers who are so different from me. They cannot understand what I've been through those many years I spent searching for a reason for living. I feel like such an outsider. It's true; these emotions are of my own making. I have to say that everyone I've met has been very kind to me. They don't seem to care where I came from or what I've done. But I care. Why can't I embrace your forgiveness for myself? My heart breaks over my past mistakes. I continue to rehearse the list of all the people I hurt because of my selfish choices. In my heart and mind, I understand that you have wiped the past away in one fell swoop. Help me embrace the grace you offer me. Let me live my life beginning today. Outwardly, I have been given that new beginning. What is so ironic is that I'm allowing what's past to destroy what's present. At this rate, my future will be so peppered with regret that I'll never break free. You know how very weak I am, Lord. Come to my aid, I beg. Let your grace envelop me even now. Strengthen me; embolden me to stand against the duplicity found within my own heart. Set me free, Lord. My hope is in you; in you alone will I find the rest I crave. Amen.

The motto for people who want to redo is, "If only I knew then what I know now." We must accept that we can apply today's wisdom only to tomorrow's temptations, not to yesterday's mistakes.
—SUSAN WILKINSON IN *Getting Past Your Past*

43
Singular Success

As the mothers passed around the tentative schedule for upcoming field trips, Sarah was impressed. Not only would this group be taking monthly field trips in the county but they were also implementing a biweekly geography session for all the kids to participate in. Perhaps the most amazing aspect of this particular homeschooling group was that almost one-half of the participants were single mothers. Sarah, a married mother of four, never ceased to marvel at how these single parents were able to handle the time- and energy-consuming job of home education on top of all their other responsibilities. One single mom ran her own full-time business and schooled her daughter on site, another mom did medical transcribing at home and taught her children at her side, yet a third mother homeschooled her three children in addition to caring for her elderly parents. It was unbelievable. Despite all the personal adversities they had to overcome, each mom continued to homeschool.

As Sarah heard of their experiences, she recognized a common thread to their stories, one of determination. Every one of these mothers had purposed to homeschool their children even though the odds against them were imposing. Each of these moms made a decision to continue (or begin) homeschooling even after their respective divorces. They worked to overcome obstacles Sarah couldn't even fathom. Time constraints, lack of money, little energy, and no spousal support all came into play as these single mothers tackled homeschooling each and every day. Sarah couldn't help but admire their commitment and their courage. She didn't know whether she'd take on such an assignment were the roles reversed. But these families were proving the dismal single parent family statistics wrong and they were accomplishing it in grand style. As one of the single moms was quick to point out, when God gives the assignment, he also gives the grace.

Let us therefore draw near with confidence to the throne of grace, that we may receive mercy and may find grace to help in time of need.
—HEBREWS 4:16

Dear Lord, I'm struck by my friends' determination and their strength of purpose. What a tremendous act of faith for these mothers to act upon the calling they believe you have set before them. I am honored to call these women my friends. Indeed, their courage and stamina put my own feeble efforts to shame. I, who have a constant support, frequently grumble when problems arise. Yet these mothers have the unbelievable task of managing their homes, working for an income, and homeschooling their children alone. Each is singularly determined to create a future full of hope and opportunity for their children. This is something I will never forget. My own faith is strengthened as I watch them face setbacks with a steady calmness. Instead of reacting, they are proactive in their decisions. They have learned how to forge ahead despite countless temporary discouragements. Would that I could learn this lesson and quickly! Lord, you have been their help. Many times these moms have spoken of tear-stained pillows and midnight prayer sessions when they called out to you for deliverance. And you answered their calls. Their pleas for assistance did not go unheeded. Rather, the provisions you made astound me. We are so blessed to call upon you as father and God. Continue, I pray, to protect these mothers against harm. Make their way smooth and give them every good gift from your bounteous supply. As these moms have brought encouragement to others, allow me to offer them a hand of help or a word of hope as the need arises. From your wisdom, let every one of us speak in such a way that reveals complete confidence in you. Thank you for demonstrating your faithfulness through the lives of these families. Your constancy is such a precious gift. Amen.

> *Life is like a coin: You can spend it any way you wish, but you can only spend it once.*
> —CHERYL CORTINES IN *First Place*

44
Redeeming the Time

Dawn's fingers brushed up against her seven-year-old daughter's as they worked to hand-mix the edible peanut-butter-flavored play dough. Dawn giggled as her hands slipped around those of little Hannah, and they shared a lighthearted laugh. Thirty minutes later, Dawn was surprised to see how many animal figures her daughter had created, despite her having taken fingerfuls of play dough and gobbled it up every few minutes. There were elephants, giraffes, rhinos, tigers, and even a few attempts at creating mud-colored flamingos. Dawn sat down and admired Hannah's artwork. Then Dawn asked Hannah if they should save them to show to Daddy when he came home from work. One might have thought Dawn had offered her daughter front-row tickets to the circus for all her excitement. Hannah spent the remainder of the afternoon setting up a "petting zoo" for her display of animals. As Hannah painstakingly fixed everything "just so," Dawn watched from the sidelines and suddenly felt that familiar melancholy mood take over. Just don't think about it now, Dawn told herself fiercely. You still have another nine months before the fall. Make the most of the time you've got, she chided.

Dawn set her jaw and decided that come fall when her husband went back to school full-time and she went to work as a secretary in the elementary school, she would have her hands full enough without working herself into a state months ahead of time. Dawn tried to comfort herself with the thought that Hannah would be attending the same school where she would be employed. She could still see Hannah during the day, still keep an eye out for her. This fact alone made the idea of returning to work for the year tolerable. Dawn and her husband agreed that once he completed his master's degree, Dawn would be free to homeschool Hannah for the remainder of her school years. Dawn couldn't wait for her husband to walk across that stage with diploma in hand.

For I am convinced that neither death, nor life, nor angels, nor principalities, nor things present, nor things to come, nor powers, nor height, nor depth, nor any other created thing, shall be able to separate us from the love of God, which is in Christ Jesus our Lord.
—ROMANS 8:38–39

Dear Lord, it makes me sad to think about all I will miss next year as a homeschooling mom. This year will go by quickly, I'm sure. I suppose I'm still second-guessing our decision. I don't want our child to suffer if we've made a poor choice. Lord, I will continue to pray and ask that you give us your wisdom in this matter. When I first considered this major life change, I was overwhelmed. Then you brought a better perspective to my heart. For this, I am so grateful.

Lord, I also ask that you make this year a fruitful one. Help each one of us take full advantage of these new opportunities to learn all we can. Give us the stamina to enter unfamiliar territories and settle in without difficulty. I pray that you will surround us with your protection. Let us find good friends and make the effort to be friendly to those we encounter. Enable us to serve others with a generous spirit, and may your love shine from within our hearts. Instead of feeling sorry for ourselves, I would ask that you generate a desire to afford comfort and care to those we will meet. This new year has such possibilities. Be with us, Lord, as we strive for excellence in all things. Let nothing separate us from the knowledge that no matter where we go, you are right beside us. Thank you again for the many evidences of your benevolent grace. Amen.

Don't avoid life's Gardens of Gethsemane. Enter them. Just don't enter them alone. And while there, be honest. Pounding on the ground is permitted. Tears are allowed. And if you sweat blood, you won't be the first. Do what Jesus did; open your heart.
—MAX LUCADO IN *Traveling Light*

45
Skipping School?

With the last of the morning's errands completed, Lana breathed a sigh of relief. Perhaps for the first time in her memory, Lana had actually made it through the morning without some cashier, druggist, librarian, or postal employee giving her children the eagle eye. Invariably, one of these well-meaning adults would inquire as to why the children weren't in school. It isn't a holiday is it? Are they sick? Is your school closed for the day? Lana had heard it all. In her six years of homeschooling, she'd not only listened to the questions, she'd also picked up on the subtle inference that she was doing something wrong. No question, many adults were just flat out skeptical about the whole home-schooling movement. It constantly amazed Lana, given the state of some of the public and private schools in her area, that anyone would feel justified pointing a finger at her.

During those first couple of years, Lana felt the sting of reprisal hit hard. But after a while, she didn't seem to mind anymore. It wasn't that Lana had grown callous toward others' questions. Rather, she had grown comfortable with her position on the matter. Lana had seen the positive results with her own eyes and she didn't feel any defensiveness toward those who simply didn't understand. These days, instead of stiffening up when the expected queries came, she just smiled warmly and explained that she home-schooled her children. If someone inquired why she wasn't "home" schooling them during regular school hours, Lana would explain that flexibility was one of the greatest bene-fits of homeschooling. On given days, her children might do all their work after lunch and throughout the afternoon if they had scheduled appointments or field trips in the morning. Lana recognized that as she responded respectful-ly and kindly toward others, they in turn usually did the same.

Pursue peace with all men and the sanctification without which no one will see the Lord. See to it that no one comes short of the grace of God; that no root of bitterness springing up causes trouble, and by it many be defiled.
—HEBREWS 12:14–15

Dear Lord, today was such a milestone for me. I must write this day down in my journal. I was actually able to patiently explain all the hows and whys of homeschooling with a not particularly friendly individual. It pleases me to realize that you have brought me full circle in this area. I recall not too long ago how upset I would become when others questioned me about why my kids weren't in school. Maybe they weren't as accusing as I once believed, but I felt badgered and misun-derstood. I allowed the negativity and misunderstanding of a few people to destroy my contentment. Then I would question the wisdom of homeschooling all over again. But this day, it was different. You gave me the words to speak in answer to pointed questions. You opened my heart to converse with this stranger with gentle patience. You alone made it possible for me to share my convictions in a convincing manner. Thank you, Lord. I believe I gained an audience today and perhaps even made a friend. Oh, Lord, I am so grateful that you continue to refine and work in me. I don't often see much evidence of change within my heart, but this afternoon was different. I am greatly encouraged. And still, I also realize that every time I step through my door and enter the public arena I am opening myself up to curiosity and questions. Give me the grace to deal with each new opportunity as you would have me. Please enable me to see questions as fresh chances to share the good things you've done in our family. Let my countenance spread hope, joy, and love to everyone I encounter. Again, I give you thanks, Lord, for this blessed day. May many such profitable exchanges come to pass in the days to follow. Amen.

I think the most important thing is a life well lived. I believe a person living an honest life, a life of good character, good integrity; who loves his spouse, who does his work well, shows up on time, pays the bills—that's the gospel in the flesh.
—MAX LUCADO IN *Secrets of a Faith Well Lived*

46

The Most Precious Thing

When the clock struck 3:00 P.M., Darcy bundled up in a cumbersome wool coat and lined boots and completed her ensemble with hat and mittens. It was snowing heavily and the wind was fierce. One more time, she thought. Darcy's driveway was about one-half mile in length and their mail arrived anywhere between 12:00 P.M. and 5:00 P.M. There was no telling why their delivery was such a happenstance affair. But today's mail was important. In fact, it was a milestone of sorts. Darcy's daughter, Alexis, would be receiving her first library card. Although a plastic two-by-three-inch card wouldn't mean much to most people, it meant the world to Alexis. At eleven years old, Alexis had mastered the art of reading! Given her many disabilities, doctors told Darcy and her husband not to expect much from their daughter. If she even learned to dress herself or pick up a spoon at meal times it would be a miracle.

Don't expect too much, was the constant refrain for the first few years of Alexis's life. Day after day, Darcy worked with her daughter. They went through a grueling exercise and stretching routine each morning and evening. Darcy patiently kept at it until Alexis's muscles began to learn how to function properly. Darcy read all she could about Alexis's special problems. It didn't take long for Darcy to see small signs of progress. Though Alexis's body responded more quickly to Darcy's efforts than did her mind, Darcy never gave up. Teaching Alexis to perform simple tasks took weeks, sometimes even months. When Alexis turned nine, Darcy decided to tackle the impossible. Reading. Every afternoon, Darcy would read aloud to her daughter and then bring out a phonics book. Painstakingly, Darcy would point to a vowel and say its sound, and Alexis would repeat it. Even though it took over two years for Alexis to complete the core lesson book, she finally closed it for the last time. Darcy promised Alexis her own library card once they finished the phonics program. So today, once the mail arrived, this mother and daughter would drive to their library and Alexis would have the privilege of passing her very own library card across the checkout counter.

"For nothing will be impossible with God."
—LUKE 1:37

Dear Lord, I never thought we'd make it to this point. I am so overwhelmed with the joy of this grand accomplishment that words cannot express what I am feeling. Thank you, Lord. You made this possible. I am so very grateful for your constancy and care for my child. And for me! Now I believe that we've turned a significant corner in our lives. Year after year, you showed us the next step to take. Your grace made it doable even when I had no clue how to tackle the newest challenge. Again, I must give you thanks, Lord, for the joy I see written in my child's eyes makes all the sacrifice seem like nothing. You have made the impossible possible! Lord, I ask that as we bask in the glow of this achievement that you continue to hold your hand of encouragement out to my child. She has come so far, yet there is much more work ahead of her. Please keep your protective arms around her. Give her the stamina to keep learning. Let her not become discouraged as she encounters setbacks. And help me know how to be the best teacher for her special needs. I am honored to be her mother. I am grateful for this opportunity to introduce my dear daughter to the wonders you've created. As her tiny world broadens and expands, let your love always serve to guide her and uphold her. Thank you for loving my child and for teaching me how to do the same. Amen.

Self-pity, fixated on its own unfulfilled need for love, will not reach out and give love to anyone else. It doesn't understand that giving is receiving.
—MIKE MASON IN *The Mystery of Children*

47
Second Chances

Laurie hung up the telephone receiver quietly so as not to awaken her ten-month-old son from his nap. Listening for any sign of disturbance, Laurie carefully made her way into the family room to settle in for a few moments of solitude. With the older children outside, Laurie took full advantage of her son's habit of sleeping through the afternoon hours. As Laurie leaned deep into the cushiony rocker, she closed her eyes, not to sleep, but to pray. Her friend Dee had just gone through another couple of tough homeschooling crisis days. Dee, who had three elementary age children, pulled her kids in and out of public school more times than Laurie could remember. It seemed every fall, Dee would start off with a strong determination to homeschool and by mid-November she was falling apart. If left up to Dee, she probably would never even have entertained the thought of home educating in the first place. But Dee's sisters-in-law all homeschooled their children. Dee felt obligated, and not a little pressure, to comply with the rest of the family. From every side, Dee felt cornered, so she did her level best to live up to others' expectations of her.

Dee might not have realized it, but her friend Laurie was ready to encourage her to make the most courageous decision possible. Laurie, who had come alongside Dee and helped her through minor and major upsets, really believed that Dee wasn't suited for homeschooling. It wasn't that Laurie didn't believe in Dee's ability to succeed, rather, Laurie knew that in order to homeschool over the long haul, one must want the job. Dee didn't. Like any other vocation, homeschooling takes discipline, drive, and commitment. Dee's heart just wasn't in it. Laurie believed Dee had given it her best. Laurie prayed that Dee would accept her words in the loving context in which she meant them. Laurie would also encourage Dee to sit down with her husband and have a long heart-to-heart before any more time passed.

❧

Consider what I say, for the Lord will give you understanding in everything.
—2 TIMOTHY 2:7

Dear Lord, I want to thank you for my friend. She is one in a million. I cannot think of another woman who has sacrificed so much for her family and without complaint. Lord, though she doesn't realize it, she has become my hero of sorts. She has pushed aside her own desires and dedicated herself to homeschooling when it was the last thing she wanted to do. Every year, this brave gal does it again. True enough, from the world's perspective she may not look like the epitome of a contented homeschooling mother. But she's done her very best. I know that you are pleased with her. Lord, I need your wisdom as I approach my dear friend in love. I want her to be

*assured of my admiration and respect for her as a person and
as a mom. She is truly a marvel. I'm afraid, though, that my
words may hurt her. Lord, prepare my heart and hers to converse in a manner that is edifying to you. I want to share my
thoughts with her to help her, Lord. Please enable me to say
what must be said and to do so in a way that draws us closer
as friends. Let her not feel that I am accusing or condemning,
because I am not. I believe that you've helped me see that
perhaps homeschooling is not the best choice for her and her
children. Lord, if I am wrong, please put a seal over my lips.
Guide my words, I pray. Let nothing I say cause further discouragement or pain. Give us your grace and embrace us
with your presence as we share together. Lord, I ask that you
come alongside my friend and help her through this difficult
time. And please show me how to be the friend she longs for
in her time of need. Amen.*

> *If those who need a comeback only see our strengths, they won't
> know and they can't see that God takes brokenness and mends it.*
> —JOHN SLOAN IN *The Barnabas Way*

48
Dusting Off the Dreams

For years, Olivia wanted nothing more than to live out in the country, somewhere where she could set her hands to working in the soil and creating beauty out of barrenness. Olivia's off-and-on career as a real estate agent made her privy to the best land deals in her county. After months of looking for just the right piece of real estate, Olivia discovered the place of her dreams: ten acres, two outbuildings, a pole barn, a pond, and an aging farmhouse. It was the recipe for success in Olivia's mind. Together, Olivia and her husband visited the site several times before making an offer. Within ten weeks, Olivia was living her dream. Soon after moving in, she ordered a small stock of chickens, goats, and turkeys. "Next year, we'll expand and get a Jersey cow, too," Olivia told her friends in excitement.

With Olivia's enthusiasm and business savvy, it was to no one's surprise that she succeeded in her homesteading venture. But Olivia wasn't merely living out her personal life-long desires, she was also thinking about her children. Olivia wanted her kids to have a hand at creating something from nothing. She knew they'd thrive in the setting where outdoor chores involving caring for animals would strengthen them in countless ways. As they got up early and fed and watered each of the stock, Olivia watched her children develop an inner discipline and a stronger work ethic. When Olivia suggested they build a sod house, all the kids pitched in and followed Olivia's lead. Come planting time, Olivia taught the family how to properly cultivate the soil, plant straight rows of seeds, and how to tell the difference between the weeds and the vegetables. All in all, Olivia was tickled with their progress. She admitted that some mornings when the wind chill fell below zero it was torture getting up and outside to work. But reviewing the past year or so, Olivia couldn't conceive of a better place to enhance her kids' education.

And lovingkindness is Thine, O Lord,
For Thou does recompense a man according to his work.
—PSALM 62:12

Dear Lord, can this be real? Am I truly living out the very desires of my heart? I keep asking myself if I'm dreaming. I cannot thank you enough for allowing us the privilege of living in this wondrous place. I'm so overcome by the beauty I witness each and every day. My heart expands just thinking about the potential we have as we labor and cultivate this land. Lord, you are too good to us. I have prayed for years for just such a haven. You provided not only what I requested but far more. Amazing. Again, I cannot stop giving you thanks and praise for your bounty. We are learning so much about this fascinating world you created. Nothing is taken for granted here. Lord, I am so grateful that my children have the opportunity to get their hands dirty. I am witnessing real changes taking place in them. When we first moved, they were hesitant and unsure. Now, no job is too difficult. They jump in and give it their best effort. I pray that you continue to work within all our hearts and lives. Help us appreciate this world you created on our behalf. Open our eyes to see the beauty that surrounds us. Give us the sensitivity to drink in all the goodness in this place. And when we become weary, enable us to see past the day's labor. Strengthen us to press forward until we've completed our tasks, no matter how tiring. Lord, I am filled with wonder and thankfulness. I praise you and bless your name. You gave me a dream and you brought the fulfillment in your own way and time. I pray that I might make the most of every day you've given me, never taking anything for granted. Amen.

It's good to have knowledge—I have learned that preparation helps avoid desperation—but in the end the journey must go on and it doesn't make sense to let fear put fences around our dreams.
—Ken Duncan in *America Wide: In God We Trust*

49
Study Buddies

With an hour in between her classes, Meredith took full advantage of the time to check out the local bookstore's newest offerings for homeschooling families. Meredith was so pleased when she received the flyer in the mail inviting all homeschoolers to an open house and afternoon of free giveaways to celebrate the store's first homeschool resource department. This would save Meredith both time and money if she could locate the materials she wanted locally. Now more than ever before, every hour made a difference. Meredith was not only teaching her two teen boys at home, she was attending college in the evenings. Meredith never planned on going back to school to complete her bachelor's degree once she married and had her sons. Then again, Meredith didn't plan on becoming a single mother either.

One of the last things her ex-husband had encouraged her to do was pull the boys out of school and follow her desire to homeschool them. Then four months later, he was gone. Meredith never did quite figure out the logic of that. But the boys absolutely thrived under her tutelage, and the pain caused by their father's departure seemed to lessen as they grew into a close-knit family unit. After a few years on her own, Meredith started looking ahead. She realized that

once her sons turned eighteen all child support would stop
and her alimony payments alone wouldn't cover their family expenses. Reentering college made sense now. Meredith
met with a guidance counselor and was glad to discover
that many of her adult life experiences would be counted
toward meeting her semester hour requirements. If she
stayed with her current schedule, Meredith would graduate
from college the same time her oldest son graduated from
high school. Many days Meredith chuckled to herself as the
three of them sat at the dining room table pouring over
their respective books until dinnertime. It was on those particular days that Meredith gave thanks for the miraculous
turn of events God had orchestrated on her behalf.

*"'Test me in this,' says the Lord Almighty, 'and see if I will not
throw open the floodgates of heaven and pour out so much
blessing that you will not have room enough for it.'"*
—MALACHI 3:10

*Dear Lord, when I look back to the devastation and pain I
underwent, I can still feel the chill of despair run up my
spine. A part of me was so numbed; I couldn't comprehend it.
But that is a closed chapter now. Today I am rejoicing in
your goodness to my family. I am so grateful that I was
already involved in homeschooling before the storms hit.
Otherwise, I would never have had the courage to pull them
out of their school and bring them home on my own. Not
with the way I was feeling—defeated, depressed, and dazed.
Lord, you truly do all things well. I firmly believe because we*

were together day in and day out, we bonded in a special way. We depended upon one another and comforted each other through the worst. Again, I thank you for allowing me time to regroup with my children in the safe harbor of my home. Now I am ready to reach out and extend myself back into the professional world. I am excited to be a part of discussions and lectures where I can interact with my own peers. This has been a such a blessing to me. And I understand that you have guided me to this place to prepare me for the time when my sons leave home. I will be ready to reenter the workforce as need be. I honestly cannot conceive of a more gentle transition than you have provided for me. As I sit side by side with my own children and we work on our individual assignments, I am nothing but blessed. Thank you for seeing past my pain and for making a way for me that has brought blessing upon blessing. Amen.

Remember, anger is rooted in fear that injustice will prevail, that we won't get what we need or want, that life is not fair, or that we will be rejected again. Fear, simply put, is a lack of faith.
—ROSE SWEET IN *Healing the Heartbreak of Divorce*

50
Graduation Day

*I*t was thrilling for Mindy to enter the halls of the junior college she attended so many years earlier. She had completed the two-year legal assistant program and had gone on to get her B.A. immediately after. Although Mindy only worked in a law office for about five years, her stint as legal assistant only increased her fascination with the law. Now, some seventeen years later, Mindy almost felt like she was the one applying for admissions. After homeschooling her daughter, Brooke, for the last five years, Mindy came to appreciate the joy of learning she'd long since forgotten. It is a privilege to take the skills you have and hone them, Mindy frequently told her daughter. Mindy was confident that Brooke was ready to enter college even though she was officially still considered a senior in high school. Her entrance exams proved Mindy correct. With only a few short months until the spring semester began, Mindy decided to take the afternoon and show Brooke around the campus. It was very similar to how Mindy remembered it. New additions and renovations of course, but to Mindy not much had changed.

After their tour, Mindy and Brooke decided to stop into the cafeteria for something to drink. As they chatted about the upcoming changes looming upon the horizon, Mindy was suddenly aware of a wave of regret wash over her. These next few weeks will be my last as a homeschooling mother, she realized. How this obvious fact had taken her off guard perplexed Mindy. *We've been planning this for months, where have I been?* Suddenly unsure of how her own life would change once Brooke entered college, Mindy wanted to turn back time. It had been a joy to homeschool these past five years. To have helped Brooke overcome some of her learning difficulties and reach the point where college is a soon-to-be reality, Mindy was beyond grateful. She was sincerely happy for her daughter. But Mindy also realized that with every milestone comes a sacrifice.

"Therefore do not be anxious for tomorrow; for tomorrow will care for itself. Each day has enough trouble of its own."
—MATTHEW 6:34

Dear Lord, it's been a delightful experience being an instructor in my home. What began as a solution to an ongoing problem transformed into a blessed gift. We have grown so close during these teaching years. I feel as though I have been given the most precious commodity on earth, a loving relationship with my child. We've laughed and cried, we've worked and we've played. But most important, we learned to take life one day at a time and to trust you for the future. I still remember how we struggled when we first began homeschooling. Today we are thriving in every way possible. I am so very grateful for the strides we have achieved. And now, as a new season begins, I've no doubt that I have fully prepared my child for the challenges that lay ahead. It's me I'm concerned about. Suddenly my world is being rocked. I'm not sure of my place any longer. Without homeschooling, my time constraints are freed. Lord, I want to be wise. Help me understand what plans you have for me in the coming months and years. Show me how to make the most of each day and not fret about tomorrow. I desire to continue serving my family in any way I can. But I also see others outside of my home that could use some encouragement. Lord, let not my heart become troubled over new opportunities. Calm my mind, speak peace to my soul. I am so full of rejoicing over the accomplishments of my child that to allow personal fears to ruin my joy would be grievous indeed. Again, my words of thanks will never come close to expressing what my heart feels. I love you, Lord. I am in awe of your goodness and care toward my family and me. I commit myself to you, trusting that you will reveal your plans and purpose for me when the time is right. Amen.

> *He gives purpose to the aimless. He gives reason to the meaningless. He gives fulfillment to our emptiness. He gives light in the darkness.*
> —ANNE GRAHAM LOTZ IN *Just Give Me Jesus*

Redeeming Grace

Shannon sat with her three children snuggled up against her on both sides. At their feet lay a largish pile of books. As soon as Shannon finished reading one story-book her youngsters clamored for more. "Read it again!" they cried. "Let's get through the stack before we reread anything a second time," Shannon replied. As the children sat entranced listening to their mom read their favorites, complete with dramatic voice inflections, they oohed and aahed in all the correct places. After reading for over an hour, Shannon called it quits. "Sorry kids, it's time for you to get started on your own reading assignments." Three smiling faces beamed up at Shannon. Their secret was out. They all knew that only mom could read . . . but they enjoyed playing along with Shannon.

"OK, everyone to the kitchen table and we'll work on our long and short vowel sounds today." Three sets of feet quickly padded into the pantry area. Shannon laid out three colorfully laminated place mats with the alphabet written on them. Then she sat down with her phonics book and worked through the lesson. Even though only her old-est was truly ready to read, Shannon found it fascinating that her younger two were absorbing some of the principles along with their older sister. Shannon carefully enunciated each vowel sound, and the children repeated after her. Within a few minutes, Shannon lost her two smallest students to a container of oversized Legos in the next room. Shannon continued working through the daily practice words until her daughter grasped the newest sounds. Then she closed the book and instructed her daughter to complete her math problems she had prepared earlier. As Shannon turned to leave the room and check on her younger two, her daughter looked up and said with a straight face, "When I grow up I'm never going to get a job. I'm going to stay home and take care of kids like you do."

"Really?" Shannon smiled at her daughter's innocence. High compliments indeed.

As each one has received a special gift, employ it in serving one another, as good stewards of the manifold grace of God.
—1 PETER 4:10

Dear Lord, winning the highest award could never compare with the satisfaction I get from being a mother to my children. I would not have believed that I could be so content as I now am. Becoming a mother has truly changed me. I don't see life as I used to. The smallest, most commonplace events take my breath away. I marvel at my children's achievements. Their smiles and their laughter thoroughly win my affections. Home has become such a blessed haven for me. I am well occupied in my time. My energies are focused on teaching my children about you and your life-giving principles. I feel challenged to give the best of what I am to mold my little ones into God-honoring individuals. I cannot foresee a time when I'll ever want for anything more to complete my life. By serving and nurturing these precious souls, I am passing on a legacy of love and faith. Only as I continue to give sacrificially will they be influenced in the manner in which you desire. Lord, continue to support my cause. Help me stay constant in my goal to live each day as a good steward of both time and talents. Enable me to say no to any pursuit that might take me away from this present task. No matter how long it takes, I trust that you will be with me. In the midst of suffering and discouragement, shore me up. Let me see your face as I spend time on my knees in intercession for my beloved family. Take this life you've given me and use me as you will. For your highest glory and honor, I recommit my life and my heart's desires to you. Amen.

Praying for your children is your responsibility. Your blessing. No one will ever pray for your child as often or with the intensity you do. No one. Because no one loves your children as much as you do, and love adds fervency and frequency to prayers.
—JEANNIE ST. JOHN TAYLOR IN *How to Be a Praying Mom*

52

Community Counts

*H*eather sat hand in hand with a gathering of fifty-plus homeschooling moms. The group leader was closing the meeting in prayer. This end-of-the-school-year celebration brunch marked the completion of another successful season. Outsiders might assume that these moms were celebrating having made it through the nine-month calendar school year. But they weren't. These women were rejoicing that they had kept their commitments to community prayer and to one another. Each summer, every woman receives a commitment packet that she prayerfully fills out, signs, and seals. They then meet together once a month for a prayer retreat at which they devote one solid hour to praying for their personal goals, their homeschools, and their communities. Unlike many so-called prayer meetings, these ladies mean to do business with God. Pre-prayer chatting is not allowed. No refreshments are served. No "sharing" of any kind until the prayer hour is over. Some might view their strict adherence to the rules as overly legalistic, but these women know that the real power to effect changes comes not from talking about problems but praying through them.

Month by month, the moms pour their hearts out to God. They plead with him for strength, support, and guidance. Some will ask for physical healing and renewed emotional well-being. Others cry out for sons and daughters who are struggling in their studies. But every one of them calls upon God to continue ministering on behalf of their fellow homeschooling friends and moms. The camaraderie is breathtaking. Heather never leaves one of these prayer sessions with dry eyes. She marvels at the sacrificial love these ladies evidence toward each another. Their prayers for one another are truly poetic and their commitment continues far beyond the once-a-month hour of prayer. Heather feels blessed to know and be known by such fine women.

It is the blessing of the Lord that makes rich,
And He adds no sorrow to it.
—PROVERBS 10:22

Dear Lord, how welcome I feel when I enter into that sacred place where we gather for prayer. Before we even begin, I can sense your spirit there, dwelling in our midst. It is always a hushed, quiet mood. We women still our hearts and minds. We sweep away the debris of the day. After some silence, we are ready to address you properly. Our hearts are submissive and receptive. We open our time of prayer with gifts of thankfulness for your many blessings and provisions. Once we have given thanks, we lay our needs before your throne openly and without shame. Our cries for mercy, forgiveness, and restoration mingle with our tears. As we feel assured of your love and compassion, we intercede for our families and our communities. No one is outside the boundaries of our prayer circle. As our time grows to a close, we end in another resounding round of thanksgiving and praise. Then we step away from the warmth of such shared community and reenter our own worlds. But the goodness we gain from our time in prayer goes with us. Lord, coming before you is indeed the highest privilege. To share it with others is a joy beyond this world's measuring. It is to our good that we take these prayer retreats together, joining our hearts and souls to further your kingdom and cause. Never let us stray far from our knees, Lord. Keep us tender to the glorious mysteries of continual prayer. Beckon us back when we waver and remove the dross from our eyes when we fail to see the truth. Let us always be sensitive to the gentle tugging of the Holy Spirit and obedient to his call to pray. Remind us that Jesus never stops his work of prayer on our behalf. Teach us to emulate him in all ways, most especially in the way of prayer. Transform us, Lord, into women whose sole source of hope and strength comes directly from your hand. Amen.

For those explorers in the frontiers of faith, prayer was no little habit tacked onto the periphery of their lives—it was their lives. It was the most serious work of their most productive years.
—RICHARD J. FOSTER IN *Celebration of Discipline*

Sources

Part One: The Practice of Homeschooling

1 Elisabeth Elliot, *God's Guidance* (Grand Rapids, Mich.: Revell, 1997), p. 108.

2 Karol Ladd, *The Power of a Positive Mom* (West Monroe, La.: Howard, 2001), p. 75.

3 H. Jackson Brown Jr. and Rosemary C. Brown, *Life's Little Instructions from the Bible* (Nashville, Tenn.: Rutledge Hill Press, 2000), p. 111.

4 Jud Wilhite, *Faith That Goes the Distance* (Grand Rapids, Mich.: Baker Book House, 2002), p. 41.

5 Joseph M. Stowell, *Loving Christ* (Grand Rapids, Mich.: Zondervan, 2000), p. 98.

6 Calvin Miller, *Jesus Loves Me* (New York: Warner Books, 2002), p. 34.

7 Barbara Johnson, *Pack Up Your Gloomies in a Great Big Box* (Dallas: Word, 1993), p. 29.

8 Max Lucado, *Traveling Light for Mothers* (Nashville, Tenn.: W Publishing Group, 2002), p. 60.

9 Jim Dowling, *Meditation: The Bible Tells You How* (Colorado Springs, Colo.: NavPress, 1976), p. 96.

10 Calvin Miller, *Jesus Loves Me* (New York: Warner Books, 2002), p. 92.

11 Oswald Chambers, *My Utmost for His Highest* (Grand Rapids, Mich.: Discovery House, 1992), May 8.

Part Two: Teaching Day by Day

12 Richard J. Foster, *Celebration of Discipline* (San Francisco: HarperSanFrancisco, 1978), p. 113.

13 Ann Kroeker, *The Contemplative Mom* (Colorado Springs, Colo.: Shaw, 2000), p. 49.

14 Liz Curtis Higgs, *Really Bad Girls of the Bible* (Colorado Springs, Colo.: WaterBrook Press, 2000), p. 223.

15 J. I. Packer, *Knowing God* (Downers Grove, Ill.: InterVarsity, 1973), p. 245.

16 Jerry White, *Making Peace with Reality* (Colorado Springs, Colo.: NavPress, 2002), pp. 63–64.

17 James Emery White, *Life-Defining Moments* (Colorado Springs, Colo.: WaterBrook Press, 2001), p. 97.

18 Mark Buchanan, *Things Unseen* (Sisters, Ore.: Multnomah, 2002), p. 41.

19 Evelyn Christenson, *Lord, Change Me* (Wheaton, Ill.: Victor Books, 1979), p. 109.

Part Three: Character Development

20 Lou Priolo, *The Heart of Anger* (Amityville, N.Y.: Calvary Press, 1997), p. 33.

21 Liz Curtis Higgs, *Mad Mary: A Bad Girl from Magdala, Transformed at His Appearing* (Colorado Springs, Colo.: WaterBrook Press, 2001), p. 266.

22 Anne Graham Lotz, *Just Give Me Jesus* (Nashville, Tenn.: W Publishing Group, 2000), pp. 136–137.

23 *God's Little Devotional Journal for Women* (Tulsa, Okla.: Honor Books, 2000), p. 111.

24 Lou Priolo, *Teach Them Diligently* (Stanley, N.C.: Timeless Texts, 2000), p. 83.

25 Roy Hession, *The Calvary Road* (Fort Washington, Pa.: Christian Literature Crusade, 1950), p. 75.

26 Martha Peace, *The Excellent Wife* (Newberryport, Mass.: Focus Publishing, 1995), p. 103.

27 Elmer L. Towns, *Fasting for Spiritual Breakthrough* (Ventura, Calif.: Regal Books, 1996), p. 31.

28 Donald S. Whitney, *Ten Questions to Diagnose Your Spiritual Health* (Colorado Springs, Colo.: NavPress, 2001), p. 74.

29 Sheila Walsh, *A Love So Big* (Colorado Springs, Colo.: WaterBrook Press, 2002), p. 156.

Part Four: Challenges and Choices

30 Edward T. Welch, *When People Are Big and God Is Small* (Phillipsburg, N.J.: P & R, 1997), p. 19.

31 Max Lucado, *Traveling Light for Mothers* (Nashville, Tenn.: W Publishing Group, 2002), pp. 27, 29.

32 Mark Eddy Smith, *Tolkien's Ordinary Virtues* (Downers Grove, Ill.: InterVarsity Press, 2002), p. 59.

33 Charles Stanley, *How to Handle Adversity* (Nashville, Tenn.: Nelson, 1989), p. 123.

34 Cynthia Spell Humbert, *Deceived by Shame, Desired by God* (Colorado Springs, Colo.: NavPress, 2001), p. 202.

35 Oswald Chambers, *My Utmost for His Highest* (Grand Rapids, Mich.: Discovery House, 1992), Apr. 14.

36 Stormie Omartian, *Lord, I Want to Be Whole* (Nashville, Tenn.: Nelson, 2000), p. 221.

37 Roy Hession, *The Calvary Road* (Fort Washington, Pa.: Christian Literature Crusade, 1950), p. 22.

38 Sheila Walsh, *Living Fearlessly* (Grand Rapids, Mich.: Zondervan, 2001), p. 200.

39 Jean Lush, *Women and Stress* (Grand Rapids, Mich.: Revell, 1992), p. 239.

40 *God's Little Devotional Journal for Women* (Tulsa, Okla.: Honor Books, 2000), p. 27.

Part Five: The Perks

41 Mike Farris, quoted in Ray E. Ballmann, *The How and Why of Home Schooling* (Wheaton, Ill.: Crossway Books, 1987), p. iv.

42 Susan Wilkinson, *Getting Past Your Past* (Sisters, Ore.: Multnomah, 2000), p. 191.

43 Cheryl Cortines, quoted in Carole Lewis, *First Place* (Ventura, Calif.: Regal Books, 2001), p. 148.

44 Max Lucado, *Traveling Light* (Nashville, Tenn.: Word, 2001), p. 101.

45 Max Lucado, quoted in Christopher Coppernoll, *Secrets of a Faith Well Lived* (West Monroe, La.: Howard, 2001), pp. 164–165.

46 Mike Mason, *The Mystery of Children* (Colorado Springs, Colo.: WaterBrook Press, 2001), pp. 89–90.

47 John Sloan, *The Barnabas Way* (Colorado Springs, Colo.: WaterBrook Press, 2002), p. 61.

48 Ken Duncan, *America Wide: In God We Trust* (Wamberal, Australia: Ken Duncan Panographs, 2001), p. 21.

49 Rose Sweet, *Healing the Heartbreak of Divorce* (Peabody. Mass.: Hendrickson, 2001), p. 59.

50 Anne Graham Lotz, *Just Give Me Jesus* (Nashville, Tenn.: W Publishing Group, 2000), p. 129.

51 Jeannie St. John Taylor, *How to Be a Praying Mom* (Peabody, Mass.: Hendrickson, 2001), p. 73.

52 Richard J. Foster, *Celebration of Discipline* (San Francisco: HarperSanFrancisco, 1978), p. 31.

The Author

Michele Howe lives in La Salle, Michigan, with her husband and four children, where she has been homeschooling for twelve years. She is a book reviewer for *Publishers Weekly, CBA Marketplace,* and *CCM Magazine.* Michele has published over seven hundred articles and reviews and is the author of several books, including *Going It Alone: Meeting the Challenges of Being a Single Mom, Pilgrim Prayers for Single Mothers,* and *Prayers to Nourish a Woman's Heart.*